THE UPCYCLED SELF

THE UPCYCLED SELF

A MEMOIR ON THE ART OF BECOMING WHO WE ARE

TARIQ TROTTER AND
JASMINE MARTIN

ONE WORLD
NEW YORK

The Upcycled Self is a work of nonfiction.
Some names and identifying details have been changed.

Published in the United States by One World,
an imprint of Random House, a division of
Penguin Random House LLC, New York.

ONE WORLD and colophon are registered trademarks of
Penguin Random House LLC.

All photos are from the author's collection.

Hardback ISBN 9780593446928
Ebook ISBN 9780593446935

Printed in the United States of America on acid-free paper

oneworldlit.com
randomhousebooks.com

1 2 3 4 5 6 7 8 9

First Edition

Book design by Edwin A. Vazquez

Title page and part title art © ParinPIX-stock.adobe.com

To my parents, to Minnie, and to Rich

CONTENTS

PRELUDE

OUR LIVES ARE A RESPONSE TO THE CALL OF OUR CHILDhoods. Somewhere in the echoes of the past, we find our truest selves.

Who am I? Who are you?

Who we become is both uniquely shaped by our own choices and experiences and an artifact of the worlds that raised us. To begin to know oneself is to start the process of excavating the truth of who we are from those layers of influence. For so many of my generation, the world we came up in was one of seismic transformations: the destructive waves of drugs, violence, and incarceration that swallowed so many people we loved, and the art and beauty and hope we created in the cataclysm. But "doing the work" of finding our truest essence means taking a deeper look at all of it. It's a call-and-response. You call out into the void, "Who am I?" A chorus replies: *You are all of us.*

I am the product of people whose love propelled me out of cycles of violence that they themselves couldn't even escape. I'm also a child of Philadelphia, Pennsylvania, specifically the Philadelphia of the 1970s and 1980s. The values that city stamps on its youth are like brands seared into our flesh. Philadelphia is a city between worlds, ninety minutes south of New York City and four hours north of the Mason-Dixon Line. Our history leaks a particular radiation into the blood of those born within its city limits. Loyalty, fight, pride, honor.

Every piece of my environment contributed to the shaping of my character.

Mine is a communally built self. We are never simply "self-made."

THE WORK OF UNDERSTANDING our own humanity begins by returning complexity to the people who shaped us, in lieu of granting sainthood. Parents, grandparents, aunts and uncles, teachers, friends, even betrayers—in my memories now, they go from being the superheroes and villains of my childhood to mere mortals, struggling with the same dependencies and decisions as I do, and under even greater stress. The choices they made influence my own, then and now, until I consciously decide differently. Maybe this sounds familiar to you—you may see yourself in this story of going from the judge and jury of those who raised you to their simple witness, or maybe even their advocate. You might see your people in the truths of my own. Maybe as I reveal my family, in all their power and beauty and weakness and failure, you'll learn to love yours a little harder, too. Maybe as I reveal myself, in all my truth and fear and inspiration and complications, you'll go searching for yourself a little harder too.

What if we chased the threads running through the quilted patterns of our lives and pulled them. What if we trusted that tugging at them wouldn't make us less, wouldn't ruin the tapestry. What if we totally let them come apart at the seams, undid the stitches of ourselves that no longer served us, forgave them, and wove new legacies of old scraps, like Gee's Bend quilters creating intricate arrays steeped in our own history.

What if we trusted the upcycle?

IF WE DO THIS WORK for and with and in ourselves, how will our world begin to change? Will we be more compassionate? As we heal ourselves, recognize, grieve, and release the cycles of brokenness we've inherited and often pass on, can we more patiently and gingerly handle those who are cracked and sharp around the edges? So many of us learned to hunch ourselves in the face of rejection and negation and deprivation. What if we straightened our spines, fixed every vertebra? We are all worthy of restoration, of visibility, of dignity. Our humanity matters.

It's not easy to upcycle yourself. It's harder still to show how you did it. But I'll try. For the ones who asked and for the ones who need to know and for the generation coming after.

We are so used to hiding in shame, deliberately discarding the parts of ourselves that make us exiles. Casting away what is unapproved, hiding it in half truths, repressing our unintegrated shadows until they come pouring back out of us like ghosts on All Saints' Day. But facing those shadows is how you heal from life. Here is how you accept and integrate all of the broken pieces of you, jagged from change and consequence. Take them up and dust them off. Consider them, one by one. Be brave enough to love and let go what is no longer needed for this phase of your life. Piece back together what is foundational and give it a home. Reintegrate them and put them to use. They belong to you. They are you.

The upcycled self.

PART I

WHO ARE YOUR PEOPLE

DESTRUCTION
CAN COME IN
AN INSTANT.

CHAPTER 1
THE FIRE

THE STORY OF MY LIFE STARTS WITH THE FIRE. A LOT OF people know I burned down my family's home when I was six years old, but are not aware of the magnitude of that moment—and all that began to unravel after it. That, I have never spoken of publicly, and rarely even to those closest to me.

You sometimes hear stories about people who have "lost it all" and rebuilt their lives, but what I learned at a young age is that sometimes shit is just lost forever, or the cracks are so bad the building blocks never quite Lego-fit the way they once did. We lost everything we had in that fire. Yes, material goods are just "things," but the things we collect and value—especially when we're young, or broke, or struggling—are extensions of who we are. Our visible, tangible losses, then, represent something deeper. In the fire, we lost ourselves.

No one ever blamed me. My mother offered enormous grace, knowing that I was just a child. But once you've burned down your home, everything else is small in comparison. That experience of total loss became the basis of all that I am. Even though my mother can't see that now.

—

BORN CASSANDRA "CASSIE" GOLDSMITH, my mother changed her name to Trotter and added a Muslim name, Saaliha, when she married my father, Thomas Lynwood Trotter. At the time of the fire, my mother was almost thirty years old with two sons, having finally escaped the negligence of the projects for the safety and greener pastures of middle-class Mount Airy. She, my older half-brother, Keith, and I lived on the 1100 block of East Sharpnack Street, a row home in a city whose architecture tells nuanced stories of class, race, and legacy. Philly is known for its row houses—conjoined structures sharing a block-long black-tarred roof and gray pebbled-concrete sidewalk—but there exist subtle differences depending on the presence (or absence) of a front porch, stoop, or lawn. North of North Philly and bordered by Germantown, Chestnut Hill, Cheltenham, and Olney, Mount Airy row homes not only had porches, they shared long, lush grass plots in the front. It wasn't exactly suburbia, but for us, coming from South Philly, the move to Mount Airy cued the theme song from *The Jeffersons*. *Well, we're moving on up . . .*

We rented the house from my great-aunt Vivian, "Aunt Viv" to me. Aunt Viv lived in South Philly but owned properties throughout the city. She was the younger sister of my maternal grandmother, Minnie, but so close in age to my mom that the two of them were like sisters themselves. Viv rented it to us, but for all intents and purposes, given all the sharing and overlap in our family, that house belonged to my mother. It wasn't fancy, but it was the house we needed, neat and clean with some beautiful pieces inside. We had a hi-fi component set with a radio, an eight-track player, and a record player. My mother always had the hi-fi going, whether we were entertaining or home alone. The songs and sounds from that unbroken musical flow still stick with me. Our furniture was velvet, burgundy and gold, and the blue low carpeting went wall to wall on the house's main floor, stopping at the vinyl-tiled kitchen. We had a finished basement with a movie projector, which is where my half-brother spent a lot of his time. I had a complete bedroom set with a huge closet; its sliding door took up an entire wall. I even had my own television in the room. Like I said: we had things, and the things reflected something back to us about who we were, who we aspired to be. Every item in that house—the headboard that matched the dresser in my bedroom, the elegant china cabinet in the dining room, the way the hi-fi component set lifted up on its mechanical gears—is etched in my memory, cataloged in a list of the lost. But I can't remember any of it without a feeling of dread, knowing every item was doomed to vanish in smoke and flames.

When I was around four or five, I once took a glass of water and poured it slowly into the back of the television set in my room. It was one of those big-back TVs that had all these tubes and wires crisscrossing in and out of each other, all kinds of things going on in the back. The water trickled through the vents, but the set didn't catch fire. It smoked. And I liked that smell, the scent of wires being burned out. It was mysterious and electric and intensely satisfying.

Pouring water into a television wasn't an act of destruction, but of discovery. Left to my own devices I would conduct various small experiments at home, fueled by my intense curiosity and imagination and a never-ending desire to understand cause and consequence.

I also loved waging war with the plastic military figurines we called army men. My cousin Shawn, Aunt Viv's youngest son but only two years older than me, would come over and, with each *BOOM! POW!* explosion of a tank, bomb, or rifle shot in our imaginary battles, we would press the plastic faces of our soldiers into the flame from a lighter until they melted into camo-green mounds.

Smoke. Fire.

On this day, Shawn and I were warring with our army men on the third floor, in my mom's room at the very front of the house. Eventually Shawn left, but the war continued as I played alone, the omnipotent deliverer of good or evil to these plastic soldiers, fire in hand via a red lighter with a black metal hood. It fit squarely in the center of my six-year-old palm. But it had been hours of play and the metal on the lighter's top was too hot, burning my thumb. I jerked reactively, tossing the lighter away, but this was before the era of childproof flints, before the days when the removal of a finger meant that the flame would go out. On this day the fire only flickered on its short journey from my palm to the blue carpet at the base of my mom's golden drapes, on a day before the days when fabrics were treated with flame retardant.

The lighter landed. Flames shot up.

I didn't run. This seems ridiculous in retrospect, but instead of running, I tried to put the fire out. I knew that water put out fires, but I had no idea of the volume of water required. I very calmly stood up and pulled the green cap off the Niagara Spray Starch can in the corner of my mom's bedroom. I walked to the hall bathroom next door and filled it up with water, returned to the scene, and threw that capful of water into the fire. The flames drank it in, only seeming to get bigger. Seeing that my best efforts had failed and were of no assistance whatsoever, I set the cap down, turned, and calmly walked out the room and descended the stairs.

As I reached the bottom step, Keith and James—the latter

my mom's boyfriend at the time—came running up from the basement.

"I smell smoke, what's going on?" James yelled out at me.

"There's a fire upstairs," I said, just on some chill shit. We all looked up—the fire had already engulfed the whole landing area. James called the fire department and we all calmly walked out of the house. Once the fire trucks pulled up, James and I jumped in his orange Thunderbird to go pick up my mom, who was at a doctor's visit, leaving Keith behind. I could see the black smoke rising into the sky for blocks and blocks as we drove away, a plume above the lines of low-storied row houses. The image would come back to my mind years later when, in an unprecedented move, the city's police department dropped a bomb on the MOVE communal row home, starting a blaze that engulfed a subsequent sixty-one additional properties in a horrible conflagration that could be seen for miles around.*

It wasn't until we returned to the scene with my mom that the full force of the event struck me. As we turned down our street, a vision of chaos and destruction unfolded. It blew my young mind to see our house at the center of this world of police cars and firetrucks, smoke and smolder, red and blue and white lights flashing. As I took in the intensity of the scene in front of me, the gravity of the situation set in on me.

* MOVE was a Philadelphia-based Black liberation group self-described as a "back-to-nature" movement. Its members lived in a row home together, and on May 13, 1985, after a daylong standoff between police and MOVE members inside the house, the Philadelphia police department bombed the building from the air, marking the first time a U.S. city had ever bombed itself. Eleven MOVE members were killed inside, including women and children. Police prevented the fire department from controlling the blaze, which resulted in the destruction of the other sixty-one properties.

What the fuck did you do?

To make matters worse, we didn't see my half-brother at first until we finally found him: in the back of one of the police cars. While we were gone, firefighters had put out the fire and then walked through the house, making sure it was fully extinguished. When the firefighters emerged, Keith accused them of intentionally smashing photo frames and stealing valuables like jewelry and rare collectible coins. A scuffle broke out on the front yard, my half-brother rolling around with one of the firefighters, and he was arrested on the spot. This first charge would signal the beginning of Keith's entangled history with the prison-industrial complex. He would spend the rest of his adult life in and out of prison. On that day, he was in his early teens.

My mother, surveying it all, was eerily calm. Standing in front of our home, the last wisps of smoke floating from the blacked-out upper window, one child's hand in hers and another child already gone, her reaction that night taught me one of the most valuable lessons I've ever learned: so long as we are okay and we are safe, nothing else matters. Things might be lost forever, but even when our souls are broken, burned, or misplaced, they can be rebuilt, pieced back together, quilted into something new, maybe something beautiful. As long as we stuck together, my mom seemed to say, staring at our hollowed house with my hand in hers, we'd be okay.

We were never able to replace all the things we lost that day. I still remember the clothes I lost to the acridity of smoke and mildew from water, the photographs of bygone souls burned, the irreplaceable valuables never again found. I lost the security of a family home, the people I loved united under one roof, every room and hall decorated with our very identities in ways no home of ours would ever be again. What I didn't know yet was the greater loss of that night: my mother would never again be the same confident woman who woke up that morning in a clean, neat house on Sharpnack Street in Mount Airy. That woman was lost, too.

But there, standing hand in hand in the shadow of a burning house, we believed that we would be okay. In the face of a wall of fire, we found a new center.

WE WEREN'T ABLE to move back into what was left of the crib for some weeks, and once we did we had to make our home in the basement. The whole house carried the strong smell of smoke and char, so it wasn't long before we had to move out completely. For a while we surfed from sofa to sofa in the homes of Aunt Viv and other family members. While I was always an introverted kid who saw the world in different colors than the people around me, I folded even deeper into myself after that day. I became quieter, more reserved.

With Keith now gone, sent off to some juvenile facility, all my mom and I had was each other, on our own and without shit to our name. Her unspoken promise to me was that she wasn't going to let that stop her from providing for me, or stop me from thriving in school, in my art, in all of my young life. I watched my mom figuring out how exactly to rebuild us, while I tried to figure out how to help.

We were ignorant of the enormity of the event and oblivious of what lay ahead. But that fire was the ruthless clearing element of life as we had known it. And the unforgettable foundation on which the rest of my life would be built.

KEEP A LIST,
CHECK IT TWICE,
AND STAY FLY.

CHAPTER 2
CASSANDRA "CASSIE" SAALIHA TROTTER

***I WAS A WOMAN** who defied all definitions and I wanted to do that for my kids. Doing it for me took me down some hard paths [filled with] struggles I never even showed my son. Couldn't show him, wanted to protect him from. That was my journey, I realize now, my fate, to hold those blows. To protect him from all that was ugly. To take those hits myself so he wouldn't have to. Not like some lesson—don't water me down to that—but I was his only love. I loved him with everything in me and I wanted to give him the best. Like pushing him to it, giving your baby to the people standing by the tracks when you're stuck in those tracks and can't get up, but you gotta get your baby out, got to let him live. That's all I wanted for Tariq. I needed and wanted Tariq to survive. And his grandmother knew, she knew. She knew what I was trying to do, and she helped push him even when my hands couldn't reach. We were all pushing him, you see; we all had to get him out. We tried to give him the best of ourselves, but that was hard, we were so young and so human, you must tell him that. But Tariq never looked at me with judgment.*

Yes, I would come back for those checks every month,

but he greeted me with love in his eyes, that unconditional pure love that wasn't tainted by anything in this world, and I needed that. Needed it every month, and after the things I had done and seen. It was like jihad, a pilgrimage to love itself, to see my son. Not like church, but a blessing all the same, once a month, to see him, know he was well. It was a ritual for me, one that I could count on. I could always count on him to love me, tell him that.

After the fire, I came undone a bit. There was so much of me wrapped up in that house. So much lost. He didn't see it, or only saw a portion, but we lost so much that day. I couldn't be mad at him; he was a child. It was my failing. I cried to my boyfriend that day and to my mother, Minnie, I cried. She had to help piece me back together so I could piece [Tariq]. We tried to make it work in that house given all that I had put into it, all that Viv had given us, but the smoke was too much. The stench was in everything. It ruined things.

He knew. Tariq did. He doesn't talk about it because he knew what he had done. Notice how he skips over that every time? Goes straight to where we lived afterwards? The guilt he felt was gripping him, my little boy. He was struggling with some grown-up perceptions, he could see my stress and I think that broke him open inside. That's when he got that job, when he heard me wondering out loud about where we were going to live. But his little self was so confused about what to do after that.

He can carry on as if it didn't affect him, but I knew. It broke both of us. That's when rent parties became a thing, when the drugs became more of a release for me. It set me back because what man wants to come over a woman's house that isn't done? Isn't hers, isn't right? I had men around him that helped us, helped him, until I lost it all. But I was also determined, we were all determined, to push him out and up, out and up, out and up. We had to push that baby up out of there and into some good places and I think he wanted that for himself, too.

I LOVED HIS FATHER SO MUCH. *Tommy saw something better in me, he saved me from all that was confining me, holding me back. That's why I tried to keep Tariq from my mother's Christianity, because those were the things that had limited me. But Tommy saw the light inside me. He was intelligent, sharp, he pushed and pulled me out of where I was stuck. I loved that house we had together because it was ours. He made sure I was good, and I never had a man take care of me like that. Not my daddy, he wasn't shit, or at least that's what my mother would say. I felt the same way about men like my father, men who had never been there for me. And then here comes Tommy. Saw me trying to make it work, pulling and shifting things around to make them happen. Me already with one little boy, Keith, that I couldn't manage, but Tommy loved me.*

I pushed Tariq. Because that's what Tommy would have wanted. His son, his namesake, his legacy. He was so proud of that baby. So proud to have a son. Fatherhood changed something in Tommy. I would watch him on the bed with Tariq on his chest, lifting his head. There was pure love. I had never been so proud to be a woman. Me and Tommy, we had our fights, but don't judge [us]. I was hard on him and him on me and sometimes that's just what happens with a man and a woman. That was our reality and that's what was going on. But that love and that peace was what I felt most of the time.

Tommy had a vision for our lives that I deeply respected. When he was killed, I knew what I had to do for Tariq. I had to push him the way his father was pushing himself, the way that he would have wanted his son pushed. All that and more for that baby boy and I loved it, the responsibility of it. All. Maintaining Tommy's legacy and upholding those standards. Yes, Faheem came to us and stayed close, became a protector. He loved Tariq too and that was the thing I needed, a man that would love that boy. Not hit him or hurt him, but love him like Tommy loved him and would have loved him. I needed him strong and tender. It was hard to find. But now that's the kind of father Tariq has become to my grandchildren, strong and tender, even when it's hard.

MY MOTHER, CASSIE, was the only child of my grandmother, Minnie. Minnie's siblings were Cassie's village, creating a foundation of loyalty, love, and violence that she depended on and that helped see us through those years after the fire as we tried to make a new world for ourselves.

Cassie was short with a huge presence; I would peep how she was always well dressed and at the center of her circle of friends. But she contained multitudes. She was also a hustler: check fraud, credit card scams, and petty theft were all options when she needed to provide for us. She would get caught, give the police a fake name, and use her one jail call to hit Aunt Viv, Minnie's sister, who would in turn call my cousin Shawn's dad, Eddie G—who worked as a prison guard—to get my mom out before her fingerprints came back from the physical matching system weeks later and her cover was blown. I didn't hear all these calls. I only knew that my mother refused to let me go without.

Even before the fire my mom was a fighter, on some "where there's a will, there's a way," and she always had a will. She would do whatever she had to do to make it possible for me to do whatever I had to do. I wanted to go on a trip. I wanted to take art classes—anything, small or large, that you could think of, Mom was on it, because she wanted to ensure that I was exposed to as much of the good of the world as possible, that I stayed as alert to beauty and as hungry to learn as she was.

We had, in the old house, a collection of vinyl records and encyclopedias—back then you could mail-order a set, or sometimes salesmen in their well-tailored, distinctive suits would come right to your door. It wasn't just us. Everybody we knew had encyclopedias and a record collection, it was the then-equivalent of having the internet. Her music collection was extensive and included compilations like *The Best of the Sixties* and *The Best of Doo-Wop,* which we used to play all day in that big wooden entertainment center. When Mom had guests over I would come down the steps in my good suits, doing my best James Brown or Earth, Wind & Fire routines for her and her friends, just trying to make her laugh and be in the conversation. She had people over pretty regularly, before the fire.

THEN THERE WERE THE MEN. I never knew my father; I was just a baby when he died. But over many years and varied accounts I pieced together an outline of a character whose details have been colored in from sometimes skewed perspectives. There was an odyssey of a letter that my half-brother, Keith, wrote me during one of his many stints in prison. In it he recounted the complexities of my dad, layered in with his admiration: Tommy Trotter was a good guy, respectable, clean-cut, and one that parents would welcome in their home to date their daughters. Keith's memories honor my father's decision to marry my mother and move her and her existing son out of the projects after she became pregnant with me. They reveal the depth of my father's provider mentality: *by any means necessary*. My father ran every scam known and surrounded himself with other hustlers, but the difference between him and them was his intelligence and his attitude. They feared him, and knew that he was out of their control.

What stood out from Keith's letter, though, was what he witnessed of Thomas Trotter: that he was a straight gangster, obsessed with the TV show *The Untouchables* and constantly emulating the show's mob characters. Three-piece suits were topped with Borsalino hats, accented with shiny shoes, and finished off with a cashmere overcoat over his classic shoulder holster. Apparently, he would also chew raw garlic as if it were gum to toughen himself up. Either way, he loved and protected my mother in a manner that gave her a profound confidence and clarity that no one could ever take away. After Tommy, no one could handle Cassie, who became "too fast and too slick for even the slickest nigga."

AFTER MY FATHER'S DEATH and a considerable mourning period, my mother began to date again. Some of my earliest memories of life in the years before the fire are of those men. And the normality of their abuse.

Two stood out to me. The most prominent recollection is of a man named James Black, the same James that was home with us when I burned down our house. He had a shiny, '80s-style texturized, curly-Afro type jawn, wore gold chains and big collars and pinky rings, had a couple of gold teeth. He referred to himself as a Geechee, so that's what we called him, too.* And his family was from down South, as most of our families were, but . . . he was a big-collar-wearing, Geechee-type nigga. James Black had an identical twin brother named Richard. I actually grew up calling Richard's children my cousins, not because my mom was dealing with the brother of their father, but because my mom and their mom were really tight friends and both our grandmothers were named Minnie and they hung out together, too. So, in typical Black community shorthand, they were my cousins.

In Philly at that time, the resounding belief was that women needed to find a man with a "good job"—one with benefits, insurance, and a steady and dependable paycheck for honest work. A job at UPS or the post office was the classic good job. Working on the docks at the waterfront was also considered a good job, because you could get into the union, which ensured job security. A man unloading ships or working at the food center to load produce or meat onto trucks was a catch. James was a longshoreman and therefore in demand. He drove a metallic-orange Ford Thunderbird with these soft Ultrasuede seats. Riding around with James, I learned how to get around the city, the ins and outs of Philly side streets and the shortcuts to take to avoid Broad while still getting from one end of the city to the other. I discovered how to find my bearings in the bowels of Philly while peering out of the little backseat window of that Thunderbird.

James was a cool enough dude until he wasn't. His laid-back air would switch to a threatening, aggressive, controlling side. Once he and Mom got into an argument outside of

* "Geechee" refers to a small and insular community of Black Americans living in the coastal regions of the Carolinas who came together post-slavery and established cultural traditions, language, and habits directly influenced by West African tradition.

a bar in South Philly. I don't know exactly what it was about, but my mom and me had left our house, gotten into her car, and pulled up on him at some small neighborhood spot. I watched from the backseat as Mom double-parked and jumped out of our car with her slapjack—a black leather-bound handheld baton containing a small spring mechanism that allowed it to bounce back after impact—walked over to James's Thunderbird sitting outside and proceeded to fuck it up, smashing out the windows before sliding back into the front seat of our car. When he came charging out of the bar yelling, "What did you do to my car?!" she cursed him from our rolled-down passenger window: "You motherfucker [or whatever], you did [something, probably fucked around with somebody that she knew]." He popped open the door of our car—which at the time was a Mercury Cougar, mostly brown except for the passenger-side door and most of the hood; they were bluish gray and white, the color of car primer, ready for a paint job but never painted and probably never intended to be, like the car had vitiligo—and hopped inside and started choking my mom. I tried to come to her defense and jump on his back, but it was a losing battle. He was a big Geechee down-south longshoreman old dude and I was only six years old, so he manhandled me and slapped me back into my seat. I remember him saying, "Little nigga!" just as he hit me—and I think that's the first time I recall being called a nigga. It couldn't have been my first time hearing it, but it was my first time being called a nigga by a Black person, and I remember being completely offended. His tone made me feel really insulted.

Eventually, the brawl ended and we left. My mom was crying and shaking as we drove through dimly lit Philly streets back home. But she let James keep coming around. I never fucked with him from that point on, despite him bringing groceries and giving me ten- and twenty-dollar bills. When he came around, I knew we were going to have good grub, there would be lunch meat to make sandwiches, cereal and milk in the morning, 7 Up and fruit punch, Entenmann's cakes, and other sweet-tooth things. Still, I didn't like him. I didn't care if that Geechee down-south longshoreman old dude never came back, even if we starved. He became a name on my list, the earliest, and far more serious, version of the Irk List I sometimes read out on *Fallon* now: the list of the things in life that annoy me. Back then, the list found its home inside my mom's encyclopedia sets: on the last page of the A volume I wrote the names of the people that I planned to exact my revenge upon, and James Black's name was written right after whoever killed my dad.

The second memory is of another guy whose presence was a pillar, of sorts, in our life. He was a Muslim whose government name was Grady Sharp. I've always thought about how there could only be a "Grady Sharp" in the '70s, like on the last day of 1979 someone laid down a moratorium on Grady Sharps, just retired the name, "No more Gradys, no more Sharps, it's the '80s now"—but in the community we called him Brother Faheem.

Brother Faheem was clean-cut. He wore nice coats and kufis or flat newsboy caps like you see on *Peaky Blinders*, although back then we called that style of hat "Jeffs." He completed the look with high-waisted, tailor-made slacks with pleats, and cool shoes. I believe a lot of my affinity for style and fashion is genetic—my mom had always been stylish, my grandmother was stylish, and my father was the son of Joseph Clifton Trotter, a North Philadelphia haberdasher who owned a shop where he would sell small accessories for men, but would also steam, re-blacken, and clean their hats, and shine their shoes. My dad grew up in that shop, and when they were old enough, he and his brothers worked there. Knowing this history solidified my love of hats and maintaining a certain sartorial flair—but another part of my fashion sense came from seeing Faheem come and go, looking super sharp. I don't know how he paid for them, but Brother Faheem got me the first dope coats that I owned: double-breasted tweed and camel coats from Geoffrey Beene or whichever designer was hot. I was fly, like I had my own little Geoffrey Beene store in my large closet. And he got me my own small hats to sport when I was about five, variations on the newsboy called Apple Jacks.

So much of my style, even to this day, came from looking up to Brother Faheem, and those fly looks I lost in the fire. My youngest son, Tarik, dresses the same: everything I can find that reminds me of what I wore when I was five and six, he now has in his closet—even though he grows so fast that sometimes he doesn't even get to wear the clothes before the season changes. These were pieces that I treasured, a whole aesthetic that made me feel cared for and put me in communion with the adults in my life. When we went back into the house after the fire to save what we could, none of the clothes were salvageable. It took some time—years—before I could get fly again, before I could reclaim that piece of myself that aligned with my lineage.

But even in our time with Brother Faheem, violence was never far from my mother. There was a key night when everything changed. I waited up with my half-brother for Mom and Brother Faheem to come home from an evening out. They had gone out to the fights, to watch the local boxing matches. These fights weren't especially glamorous—this was Philly not Vegas—but it was still a special event that called for starched and pressed evening attire. When they left that night, all they told me was, "We're going to the fights."

When they came home, Faheem's collar was fucked up, crunched and stretched and in a state of disarray, and my mom had a seriously black eye, bruised and swollen. And in my naïveté, I went to bed that night under the impression that when you go to the fights, the audience has to participate, too. I thought when you go to the fights, everybody fights.

Later, I overheard my mom talking on the phone with one of her girlfriends about how Faheem had hit her. My guess was that they got into a heated conversation at the fight and my mom took a tone that made Faheem feel slighted or disrespected, and he hit her in her face. Though I never looked at him in the same way, I didn't add Faheem's name to my list in the encyclopedia. He had done a lot for me, and I think not witnessing his violence directly, only hearing and guessing what that whole interaction might have been, helped to lessen the depth of my disdain. Between these two men in my mom's life and then my half-brother—who even before he was arrested at the fire, at twelve or thirteen years old, would be brawling with my mom like people you see on WorldStar, breaking furniture, rolling all around the floor, getting into very nasty physical fights—I realized at a very young age that I'd have to protect my mother as much as I possibly could. We were all we had.

MY MOTHER HAD TO piece her life together over and over again, especially as a woman brave enough to choose her own path in the turmoil of the '60s, '70s, and '80s in Philadelphia. From the loss of my father to me burning the house down, to her first son's constant incarceration, to the violence that surrounded her like a haunting destiny, there was never a straight path for her; her survival was a feat of tricky navigation. But love was at her core, radiating out from the deepest parts of her soul and coloring her every interaction and intention. Cassie lived her life fully, with equal amounts laughter and tears and pain. All to the brim. She could see past the bane of this realm and maintain a pureness and clarity in her vision of who she was, who I was, and who she wanted me to be. She was the one who first saw the importance of art in my life and both enabled and fostered it, loved my own artistic vision, knowing that it would be my saving grace. To her, my imagination was a precious gift to be honed, a blessing from the spiritual realms that allowed me to see the world with different retinas.

When picking up the pieces of a shattered reality, love is an absolutely vital place to start. It is the force that moves the soul through dimensions, the permeating energy that flows in and through all that we are and will be. For my mother and me, love was a promise: to love each other still; to love each other despite; to love each other through; to even love each other because of all that we were and would become. In that field of energy we learned how to navigate the actual and cultivate the potential, while surviving a world that tried to choke out all possibility. Through her vision and faith and love, our story—the tale of two lives inflected with violence, tragedy, and loss, but forever connected and interwoven—became our strength. I will always love my mother, unconditionally, for that.

AWAKEN TO BEAUTY,
A NEW PERSPECTIVE.

CHAPTER 3
A CREATIVE RECKONING

ART SAVED ME.

Art was a running stream of consciousness and a quiet escape, a way of leaning more deeply into myself. Developing my eye and perspective allowed me to respond to a constantly shifting world, engage with it in ways that felt distinct to me, under my creative control.

Music flowed all around me. Hip-hop arrived in full force when I was just a kid, its lyrics and rhythms transforming the sound of our streets. Gospel came through the faithful traditions and incessant prayers of my grandmother. The wails and woes of doo-wop and blues colored the laughter and libations in our living room on Friday nights. But visual art—that was mine. It was my private portal to worlds unknown to me. Drawing, painting, tagging, shading were my tools for carving imitations of life and sculpting my own distinct visions.

Before they were lost to the fire, my mother's encyclopedias would house my innermost thoughts. The first couple of blank pages at the beginning of her World Books and the last few at the end were my first canvases and journals. The *A* volume was where I kept my irk list. But in volumes *B* to *Z*,

I would draw pictures and write down everything—random thoughts, deep contemplations, agitations and frustrations—that my hyperaware mind landed on. Drawing wasn't just an act of expression, it was also an act of retention: it became a way to lock in concepts and experiences I struggled to understand.

My cousin Shawn and I would have competitions to see who could best re-create the images we wondered at in those encyclopedias. Lying on the carpet, we'd look through pictures in the massive volumes for a few minutes and then, when we found some strange creature or concept, the drawing contest would begin, both of us frantically trying to create the most accurate depiction of this thing, this animal, these people from this place that we had never even heard of before this very moment.

It was a battle.

"I bet you can't draw a platypus."

"What the hell is a platypus?"

"Look in the encyclopedia!"

And we'd hurriedly flip pages to find the image and rush to draw it, desperate to capture this swimming duck-fish the best with some semblance of resemblance. I'd draw one, Shawn would draw one, and we would take it to my half-brother or Shawn's brother or somebody's mom—whoever was older and around—and it would be a screaming, who-can-hype-their-shit-the-loudest match.

"Yo, what you think? Which one of these is better?!!"

"His doesn't even have a FACE, what are those eyes??"

"Nah nah nah, look at this jawn, you can see the mouth right there! See that?!"

And whoever won by verdict of outside judgment walked away with bragging rights. Shawn would try to win off his charisma and big mouth alone, knowing damn well that my drawing was usually better. But then, no matter who won, the loser would be like, "Ah, man, you got that. You got that . . . Well, I bet you can't beat me again!" And we would race back to the pages to find new images to imitate (or, in Shawn's case, visually mutilate). As we grew older, our competitions evolved into who could write the best rap using words out of the dictionary:

"I bet you can't use 'emulate,' 'perplex,' 'kingdom,' AND 'poisonous orangutan' in a rhyme," I'd say.

"A rhyme? I could write a rhyme with every word out of the dictionary," he'd retort.

"Alright, do it!"

AND WE WOULD WRITE our verses and then see whose rap was better, jockeying each other on the whole time. The encyclopedia, the dictionary, and just competing with him—those were the beginnings of me becoming a visual artist and an emcee.

My mother was compassionate and supportive about my art-making—and slightly but thoroughly annoyed that we were riddling her encyclopedias with pen-and-ink marks. Honestly, the same exact way I would feel if my kids kept doing that shit.

"Tariq—all you have to do is ask, and I will get you art supplies. You know we can go right to the drugstore. Why don't you go get a sketchbook? I'm going to take you to get a sketchbook, a sketchpad or whatever—so you stop writing in my damn books."

We didn't really celebrate the Christian holidays because we were Muslim, but my mother didn't want me to go without when other kids were getting gifts. So, she would give me things that were small and inexpensive, just not under some gilded, lit-up Christmas tree or in some paint-peeling colored-plastic-grass-filled Easter baskets. The gift would usually be a paint-by-numbers set, or some other art supplies, so she could encourage my creativity in that way. She watched me closely. When she saw I was good at painting inside the lines and putting colors together, it clicked for her—*Ah, that's something I should nurture.*

The summer of my ninth year, my mother found a way for me to attend art classes. We had just moved to South Philly and there was an art camp at the Mann Center in West Philly's Fairmount Park, about twenty minutes away, that met early in the day for a few weeks. The school bus would pick me up around eight in the morning, and I'd be at the camp from nine until noon. That same bus would later drop us off at a rendezvous point and I'd be back in the hood. That was the first time I realized that I wasn't missing anything in the streets. On those summer mornings I would go to classes, live a whole-ass life in a different world, come back, and dudes would *just* be waking up and *just* coming out of the crib. The day was just beginning on the block. That understanding alone lit the fire within me to want to do more with my art. The next summer I took those classes again and I excelled at them. Excelling at anything filled a well of confidence for me, one that I would draw from and use later. I was doing well in art, winning awards—and the entire activity was fun and took place in the park. Indoors was for rainy days or when we were working with the pottery kiln, but most of the time we were outdoors painting and working with art supplies that we couldn't afford to own in our own homes. It was just . . . *transcendent.*

It was then I began to realize all that Philly had to offer from an artistic perspective, which was part of my mother's goal in sending me. Philly is a city overflowing with art, one of the best art cities in the country despite constantly being eclipsed and overlooked thanks to our proximity to New York. From the world-renowned Philadelphia Museum of Art, which houses the work of modern artists like Duchamp, van Gogh, and Picasso, to the Pennsylvania Academy of the Fine Arts, which trained pivotal Black artists like Barkley Hendricks, Njideka Akunyili Crosby, and Henry Ossawa Tanner (whose masterpiece *The Banjo Lesson* was painted while he was in the city), Philly is an archive of art history. The city plan itself is a work of art. Some say the Masonic Founding Fathers laid it out in geometric patterns meant to imbue the city with spiritual power and creative, kinetic energy. Public schools could be a little wild, but back then we always had art classes (most of which have been cut in recent years, thanks to a lack of funding). When I was growing up, I was able to get all I needed from the city. The streets and blocks shaped my creative sensibilities and formed the cornerstone of my arts education, all orchestrated by a mother who saw the vision and cared deeply, even when it ruined her encyclopedias.

HOME IS A SAFE PLACE
TO WORK OR
TO PLAY.

CHAPTER 4
MOUNT AIRY

AFTER A FEW MONTHS OF STAYING WITH FRIENDS AND family, my mother had found us a more stable home in the sparsely furnished top floor of a duplex in Mount Airy that was owned by my father's parents, who lived in a small ranch-style home with a big garden in Willingboro, New Jersey.

I was a latchkey kid, given a graying white shoelace with my front door key knotted into its center that was draped over my head every morning and dropped back on the kitchen table every afternoon upon my return, always before my mother's 6:00 P.M. arrival from her job as a hotel housekeeper downtown. She would leave for work before the sun came up, coming home after the sun had gone down—I remember her putting that key around my neck and kissing me goodbye for the day on those gray winter mornings where your breath suspended just above your mouth, too cold and dense to go any farther. I would feed myself: Rice Krispies in the morning with the milk that I'd picked up on my way home from school the day before at the closest corner store. I'd use the small sugar shaker to release white crystals into the snap-crackle-pop treats so that when I was done eating my cereal there was a layer of the sweet substance at the bottom of the bowl to look forward to. I'd also grab lunch meat from the deli to make turkey and cheese sandwiches, or if we didn't have any bread I'd just take the lunch meat and cheese to school. Whatever we had would go into one of my lunch boxes, probably my favorite one, which was, ironically, the *Dukes of Hazzard* lunch box. It had their car, the General Lee, on the front of the box, blazing its Confederate flag. I would leave for school while it was still dark outside or while the sun was just cracking, peeking over the horizon with orange-tinted hues. Here I am, a little Black boy walking to school at dawn with my lunch box and thermos flying the flag of the slaveholding South.

On winter days my personal uniform was a navy blue parka with the orange guts and a fur hood, and when it was snowing or even just really cold, I'd wear snow pants, the kind that had the bib and the suspenders. Two pairs of socks on my feet, one pair on my hands, worn as mittens. My snow boots were wrecked, so sometimes I would wear rubber galoshes on top of my shoes, stuffing cardboard and/or two plastic bags inside them too. It was around this time that I started wearing glasses, very often with at least one cracked lens or a taped-up arm; constantly in a state of disarray.

My journey from the front door to the schoolyard started with a walk down a long driveway to Stenton Avenue, a busy, bustling street. Sometimes I would stroll, sometimes I would jog, trying not to step on any cracks in the first mile as I headed to my friend Eugene's house. His mom was a warm Latina lady who would give me hot tea with lemon and honey while I waited for Eugene to get up and get dressed for school. I was early because I'd left my own home earlier than I needed to, trying to walk out with or soon after my mother, not wanting to be sitting around the house alone.

Watching Eugene, I would often be struck with the feeling that he was extremely lucky. Even though it was just him and his mom, he still had someone there to see him off, and be there waiting to welcome him home. Sometimes I wondered why my mom wouldn't just come the fuck home before I got there. *Fuck that job.* Or, why wouldn't she at least wait to leave until after she'd seen me off to school? My life was different; I felt it distinctly and I didn't like it.

Eugene and I would walk together for that last stretch to school. Depending on the morning, we might be joined by other classmates, Steven and Milton, our small group of first-graders venturing forth like a huddle of middle-aged men marching off to work. It was easily a three-mile walk, but I never worried about the distance: Shawn and Aunt Viv and them lived a few blocks away from Eugene, so I knew I could always stop at their crib if I needed a break.

My little crew's route to school would take us past the Muslim temple that my mom and I would sometimes attend, and then a travel agency, a Chinese store, and a pizza place, the latter two spots still there on that strip to this day. Young's Deli was on the corner, and across from Young's was an optician, Philadelphia Vision Center, I think it was called. The guy who owned it would see us on our way to school: trudging in the snow, sometimes bombing his storefront with snowballs, or if the weather was nice, he'd watch us throw open his front door and jump inside, say some slick shit like "Kiss my ass!," and then run away. He knew me and my mom because we would get my eyeglasses from him. Farther down on that block was a bakery called Mom's Bakery that we would all go to for sticky buns or a doughnut, a cupcake—whatever we had enough change to get early in the morning to hold us over on those last blocks of our odyssey.

But on some days, we wouldn't make it to school at all.

Keith pulled me aside one day and told me about the times our mom dropped him off at school. He would wave goodbye to her and walk in the front door and then keep on walking right out the back door and off to freedom. Those stories stuck with me. Before that, I had no idea that not attending school was a possibility.

Milton was a latchkey kid like me, with nobody waiting for him at home and no one back at the crib to spot him outside. One day I told Milton about my discovery. "It's this thing that people do called playing hooky. Let's do it." And so it came to pass that on any given day, there was a good chance me and Milton would not complete that trip to school, especially if it was a snowy day. We played all day, made snow angels, and talked about our girlfriends. I had two of them in the first grade: Rhonda and Tanika.

Journeying through Mount Airy's grassy landscape, Milton and I would roughhouse, roll down hills, and run in fields, and in all the fun, I would often break my glasses. That was a problem, because I didn't want to keep having to explain to my mother how my glasses got all crooked, lopsided, scratched, and dirty, which might eventually lead her to finding out that I didn't go to school. So I would sometimes stop at that same optician on my way home and ask the owner: "Is there any way you could fix my glasses before I go home?" One day, he broke down and asked me, as he was fixing my frames, if there was anyone at home to meet me when I got there. I could see that his question came from a sincere place of concern, so I told him that when I got home I'd watch *Scooby-Doo* alone, waiting for my mom to come back. But, I told him, it would not be a good thing for me if my glasses were broken upon her arrival.

I don't know if he talked to my mom, or if he gave me a note to take home to her, but my mother and he came to the decision that he would let me hang out at that eyeglass store until around the time my mom would be getting home. Now, she didn't want me to stay there so late that I would be walking home when the sun was going down. But he agreed that he would fix my glasses for free if they broke, give me new glasses when I needed, and that if I ran errands and helped keep the place clean, I would get paid. So there I was, age seven with my first job: running errands, going to Young's Deli to get coffee, cleaning up the shop, and windexing down the counters until about four o'clock. Then I'd go home with my own money in my pocket. You couldn't tell me shit. Over time, I learned how to use the lens-cutting machine and eventually they let me pick out any frames I wanted. That's how I started getting fly-ass eyewear when I was in the second and third grade. Even after we moved to South Philly, I would still come up there to get dope glasses.

I WAS LEARNING about work ethic. Aside from school, every day I knew I had somewhere to be at a certain time and a job to do while I was there. It gave me a feeling of importance and value that stuck with me forever. I was more compassionate about my mom's work schedule after I gained some insight about what happens when you have a job, your responsibility to it and to the people with whom you work. Making your own schedule isn't an option. And making those little couple dollars was a way for me to begin rebuilding some of the flyness that I had lost in the fire, a way to start expressing myself through clothes and accessories like the adults that I respected and looked up to, who had the fly hats, coats, and suits to match. It also meant that I had a little bit of money for my lunches and bakery treats, without having to bother my mother for it. I could look at her then, leaving before the sun rose to go chase the same feeling, and say, "Yeah, go. Go and do your thing. You got to work." It was the beginning of me seeing her humanity and embracing my own.

The community that we had in Mount Airy—from my friends to Shawn and Aunt Viv's family to the shop owners that watched us on our route with a careful eye—was strong. We kids were in a small cocoon of familiarity that kept us safe and accountable. We were able to be children around adults who protected that innocence. But that didn't mean that people in Mount Airy wouldn't try to get one over. My situational awareness still had to be on point.

One day in second grade I was coming from my job wearing some gold frames, because by now I had graduated up to owning a couple of different pairs of glasses. This oldhead, probably nineteen or twenty, followed me from the store and, when we'd gotten far enough away, he walked up on me like, "Hey young bol, where you going?" He was walking with me now, not leaving, and asking to try on my frames. In mind I was panicking, like *Shit, this dude's going to try and take my glasses or kidnap me for them.* The lenses were prescription, but they were so nice that somebody might just pop the lenses out to have some fly-ass frames. He gave them back to me, but he wouldn't stop walking with me. I could see the wheels spinning in his head. This was the era of people getting their glasses snatched right off their face. But we're out in broad daylight on this busy avenue, so he was trying to figure out a slick way to do it. What he didn't know, though, is that this route was damn near like my own underground railroad: I could stop at any given point to go to Eugene's crib, Milton's crib, Steven's crib . . . Shawn and them. The temple. A small network of safe houses that I could enter and be surrounded by protection. I wasn't alone, even when I appeared to be.

Now he asked me again, more urgently: "Let me see your frames? Let me see them?" We had gotten to Shawn and his family's block, where Shawn, some of his friends, and his older brother Tyrone were on the corner outside. We spotted each other at the same time. They yelled out, "Hey Tariq, what you doing over there?!" and I ran right over as if they were the base in a dangerous game of tag, probably a look of death clouding my face. The dude broke out running in the opposite direction.

MY GRANDPARENTS WOULD eventually sell their house in Willingboro to move into the bottom apartment of the duplex we lived in after our first year there, in order to be close to us, and especially to me, the last living memory of their son. They were still reeling from his death, but my mom had moved on with her life. Five or six years had passed since my father died, so her relationship with her in-laws had changed. She felt stifled and watched living with them, unable to live the way she wanted to in the apartment above her dead husband's parents. Cassandra needed to do her own thing. But for now, she decided that if she was going to live with one of my grandmothers, she would prefer that it be her own mother rather than her mother-in-law.

We were still learning each other in Mount Airy, my mom and me. Cassie, trying to find her way back to herself and rebuilding a life and lifestyle that she needed for a sense of self-worth. Me, navigating the world then with innocence, curiosity, and awareness, still sheltered and newly introverted, but slowly piecing myself back together and trying to grow. Mount Airy, these walks, the neighborhood, my friends there, would all come back around later in my teens, a reunion of sorts and the beginnings of me seeing that there could be two ways to live, and even die—one filled with peace, tenacity, consistency, and independence; the other, unfocused and riddled with pain and conflict. But for now, my mother's journey took us elsewhere.

PART II

WHERE ARE YOU FROM

SANKOFA:
GO BACK AND FETCH IT.

CHAPTER 5
PHILADELPHIA, A WORLD

AROUND AGE ELEVEN OR SO, I STARTED GOING TO ART classes on Saturdays at Fleisher Art Memorial in the Italian Market neighborhood of South Philly, a couple blocks off of South Street. Me and my cousin Hammed would go together. The program gave us bus tokens to attend, but we used to sell them (or use them to explore places other than school), so instead we'd walk the twenty or thirty blocks to this escapist life of young artists. We would return to the hood at around noon, when the oldhead corner boys who were just waking up would ask us with a quiet, curious gaze, "What you got in that suitcase?" In one hand we each carried a huge art portfolio, leather-bound and half the size of our small bodies, and in the other an orange-topped fisherman's tackle box for our X-Acto knives, erasers, pencils, and other crazy art supplies. The interest our odd look sparked made us feel important.

But that moment of affirmation only hit once we were back on our block. Walking home through South Philly meant going through a couple of different hoods, and sometimes we needed to get a light jog on to get past the clumps of boys and men of various ethnicities who might be out that morning ready to confront two random Black boys looking nerdy and lost. Worse came to worst, we knew we could dip into those tackle boxes for a sharp X-Acto knife and we'd be armed, ready to flail it like a Spartan sword to keep a crowd or attacker at bay; the trick would be figuring how to get to the blade, locked in layers of thick interlocking plastic, in time. Still, we weren't scared, simply aware of the potentially dangerous nuances of the city and how quickly a morning of art-making could turn into an afternoon of ass-kicking. The veil between art and violence was thin.

I WAS NINE when we moved from Mount Airy to South Philly. I thought we lived in the hood in Mount Airy because we lived around Black folk, lower- to middle-class. But no. When we'd moved to South Philly it was like stumbling from a garden into an alternate reality: no grass, no trees, way more concrete, way more graffiti. The blocks were tighter and smaller. There were no backyards or driveways, just alleys. The front porches of Mount Airy were gone in favor of three to five marble steps connecting front doors to the sidewalk, which transformed into meeting spots for outdoor conversation in the warm months. Saturday's communal tradition in the 1960s, '70s, and '80s was for children and teenagers to sweep and scrub those stones with bleach and afterwards, on those weekend days, bodies flooded onto the black pavement radiating as much energy as the afternoon sun. The irony of lawnless lawn chairs in an area without a blade of grass to be found for miles, scattered in front of the buildings on every eighth-of-a-mile block and holding neighbors with eagle eyes. They knew who did and did not belong.

South Philly was a melting pot with very structured boundaries, divided by Broad Street, crossed by avenues and major numbered streets, but then subdivided into even smaller streets that all had their own character. For example: between the north-south-running South 4th and South 5th Streets was a narrow east-west street, McKean, with a tightly packed row of homes whose residents were nearly all white, mainly Italians, maybe some old Jewish people. But between South 5th and South 6th, on the same McKean Street, you would find only Black families. And if you keep going down to South 2nd and South 3rd Streets, still on McKean, you're now in an Irish neighborhood. Each block was governed by a specific cultural code that could shift by the time you got to the corner, the borderland where you'd encounter another community that lived by an entirely different set of truths. We had to know those boundaries, the dynamic microcosms within the larger organism. The boundaries told us who belongs where, and where we could go and where we couldn't, but there was also neutral territory we all shared: the laundromat, the bakery, the corner store. The four corners of every block were the intersectional portals where all these nationalities and races of people would meet. And for years, for the most part, everyone was able to coexist with a certain level of respect.

That itself is one of Philly's core tenets and lessons: knowing when to back the people on your block, but also knowing when to hide all prejudices and distrust in favor of unifying under a greater collective identity. It's this lesson that shapes the twin bedrocks of the city's tribal loyalty: we belong to our specific race or ethnic group, but our shared identity is Philadelphian. Eagles fan. Phillies fan. Cheesesteak lover, with very specific and often generationally passed-down preferences around its maker (Ricci's, Dalessandro's, Angelo's, Max's). Willing to boo Santa Claus or the Easter Bunny. Aggressive, vocal noncompliance in the face of mutually agreed-upon grievances. Exuberant celebration of underdog victories and heroes collectively deemed worthy.

But there were times the melting pot boiled over. During the day it was fine and cool for you to be on South 2nd Street, where the Mummers and all the Irishmen lived, as long as you were going to and from school or the market. But after night fell, the rules became far less malleable. If you crossed those boundary lines after a certain hour, knowingly or unknowingly, you'd find yourself in hostile territory. The residents would assume you're looking to start some shit, so they're going to start some shit first or ask you what the fuck you're doing down there. The equal and opposite would happen if they came through our blocks at nine or ten o'clock at night.

I suddenly had to retain the larger cues and codes of South Philly while also navigating the entirely new set of dynamics that ruled the Black section's corners. On our first night after the move to South Philly, my cousin, who had always lived in the neighborhood, grabbed me from the house to take a walk to the store. It was one block away, at the end of our street, but in the span of those few feet—from my steps to the storefront—we got into it with some dudes standing just outside the store. I had on some canvas high-top sneakers that I'm sure my mom thought were Adidas when she bought them, but they weren't. They had four stripes. And I think somebody said something slick about my 'didas like, "Yo, cuz, you got them fucking four-stripe Adidas on." He might have called them bobos, a common shot at knockoff sneakers, and that was it: my cousin just went in on him. They started fighting and it was savage. I'd seen people get into brawls on the schoolyard or around the way, like a shoving match, but not tryna kill each other, and I'm like, *Yo, how is this over me?? What did I do?* And then it dawned on me: *Oh, I guess this is how it is around here. You've got to just be ready to fuck somebody up at all times.* Dude hadn't even gotten the whole comment out about the shoes and these bols were on the ground.

But I learned that the situation could flip just as fast. The guys that we had beef with that night became two of our closest friends. The switch happened literally the next day. After that, they were our boys. I started to understand that there was this rage built up in our environment, this steam within everybody in South Philly that had to be let off. Can't have the melting pot without the pressure cooker. And as everyone carried that rage in their own way, no two people were the same, which made the explosions unpredictable. Violence could happen at the drop of a dime and even among friends. It mostly didn't come from a place of "I hate you forever, I want you dead." It was more like "Yo—I got some shit to get off my chest." And then once it's done, it's done. This was an important, nuanced lesson that gave me a different outlook about friends fighting, one that stuck with me. The intensity is what makes South Philly distinct, and it bleeds into the rest of the city, too, in area-specific ways. But it doesn't necessarily translate outside of city limits.

Later in life, I would get into arguments and fights with friends or people I worked with who didn't come from the same blocks I did. We would fight and then the fight would be over, and I wouldn't think much more about it. But for them, it would be devastating. The difference between us is that I learned how to deal with conflict in a pressure cooker, where letting off steam and responding to threats with absolute clarity were essential. Even among friends. Maybe especially among friends. Where I'm from, we'd respond to perceived acts of disrespect like, "Yo, you did this thing or said this thing that offended me—or after I'd told you previously not to do this thing, you did it again—and now I'm punching you in your fucking face. It's not like you're not my boy anymore. It's not like I'm going to let somebody else come in and punch you. I'm not going to let nobody jump on your ass. But you're going to hear me and you're going to take this L."

Every lesson isn't a good lesson. My willingness to use that aggressive, angry energy—energy that I learned as part of South Philly's nuanced code of ethics—is a mindset that has fucked up some important relationships forever. Some things we learn have to be unlearned.

SOUTH PHILLY'S DIVISIONS AND UNITY, silent understandings and pent-up rage, were all symptomatic of the changes in the city at large in the '70s and '80s. Philly was its own hotbed of unchecked chaos and unhinged jurisdiction, a dynamic that oscillated and escalated under the influence of our police commissioner turned two-term mayor, Frank Rizzo. He was Italian, from South Philly, and was adored by that community as a local legend. At the same time, he endowed the police force with brute authority that came crashing down on the heads of Black residents across the city. Growing up, I was haunted by the photos and news footage of Black and Brown men lined up in the street, stripped, and searched, one time for a notorious raid conducted on the Black Panthers. Police brutality has never felt foreign to me. As far back as I can remember, the images were routine: the cops pull up in a paddy wagon, beat somebody's ass, throw them in the back of the van, and pull off. The cops were corrupt, and under Rizzo they had the free rein to go after whomever they wanted, however they wanted. It's what I imagine it was like, on some level, to live in the Jim Crow

South. From the time I moved to South Philly, I knew to just run when the police came around. Why? Who knows? We just knew that when they pulled up, you don't want to be the motherfucker that they were going to catch and beat with a stick and throw in that van. So, I developed a deep knowledge of all the alleyway systems and the back blocks and how to navigate any neighborhood that I was in without being noticed; how to blend in as quickly and easily as possible with the flow of the area so that I didn't stand out. And it didn't matter that I wasn't guilty of anything. I wouldn't be running to get away with some specific crime. Running was for our safety. It was what we learned from our fathers, uncles, oldheads: you see the cops, you get out of there.

In our community, the cops were a kind of gang, but they weren't the only one. Organized crime was also prevalent, especially the Italian mob, whose members walked the streets of South Philly like they owned the city—and in some ways, in our small world, they did. A lot of that pride was reinforced with their South Philly paisan Rizzo being in office, too. Some of the bosses lived a couple blocks away from me.

When one group of people in our little melting pot solidified themselves into a criminal organization, it begat more—everyone else starts to think, *We need to form our own gang so that we can protect and look out for ourselves, especially against this other racially organized, criminally codified group*. So by the time I moved to South Philly, there was an organization called the Junior Black Mafia, the Black community's answer to the Italian and Irish organized crime in the neighborhood. At that point, all of these syndicates were into numbers running, prostitution, and rackets. They often frowned upon the whole drug game, at least out in the open. But almost everybody sold drugs low-key.

Crack hit at a time when the younger generation had

taken control from the Italian and Junior Black Mafias, now replaced by smaller crime collectives like the Latino organizations and the newer Southeast Asian gangs. The Cambodians and Vietnamese were an interesting case: the parents, who came over as refugees, would pick fruit, save up, open a store, and start doing okay for themselves, integrating into the city. The kids of these immigrants grew up going to public school with me and my friends, resulting in these Black-sounding, hood-ass Cambodian and Vietnamese kids. When they would get picked on, like everyone else, they cliqued up, and as we got older and deeper into the '80s, their gangs were some of the most ruthless motherfuckers, period. The Asian gangs started expanding in South Philly during that crack era, lighting shit up. The first time I saw assault rifles and other big-ass guns, they were brandished by the Vietnamese boys around the way as a distinct threat: *Don't fuck with us. We come from war.* Meanwhile, their parents were still on the humble American hustle, waking up at four-thirty every morning to load up in the vans and go pick their berries and come home, trying to get their kids to stop selling crack, trying to make enough money to get out of there and save their children from the environment they had fallen into. We lived right next to a Cambodian family who kept their own chicken coops to be self-sufficient, and whose roosters woke me up every day at the sliver of dawn. The family would get up, go pick fruit, come back, and work in the store. Then on the other side of us was a Black family who had a party in their house every day; it was pretty close to being a speakeasy, that one house where everybody would go because they sell drinks and there's music all the time.

It was wild how multicultural these few, dense blocks were—Jews and Italians and Irish and Puerto Ricans, plus the more recent mix of Cambodians and Vietnamese and immigrants from the South Pacific. But we were all South Philly; the special quality of life in that fragment of the city bonded all of us. There were moments when we celebrated that collective identity—like how *Rocky* became our superhero. The entire franchise was huge for us because it was a Philly story. I knew so many people that lived and looked like Rocky in South Philly. When I was a kid, I sold shopping bags in the Italian Market; it was the place where my grandmother took me shopping every weekend. To see this guy going from tragedy to triumph, symbolized by the route he takes in that now iconic scene, from South Philly to the Philadelphia Museum of Art, through that same Italian Market? Legendary. Even if he's not a real person.

Now, some people think of the character of Rocky as being a great white hope whose mission is to wrest the title away from a slick Black interloper. Philadelphians never saw it this way. We didn't even see him as "white": I—like most of us—saw him as South Philly Italian. And I identified with those Italians because even though they weren't Black, hailing from these small streets south of City Hall gave us a shared identity. A win for the Italians, for the mob, Rocky, all of them, was a win for me because we were all from downtown. I felt the same thing for the Irish Mummers, who would have a massive parade every year on New Year's Day. When the parade was over, they came back home and had their own celebration back in the hood. The Irish part of the neighborhood was only two blocks away from me; the Mummers Museum was walking distance from my house. So, it felt like the whole neighborhood was celebrating with them when they returned from their day of dancing, drunk and ready to party some more. On that day, I felt like a Mummer myself.

Philadelphia is a city that is no one thing. It's more a place people wind up than a destination, and those accidental arrivals come together to create a layered intersection of histories, memories, and heritages. Learning to navigate its subtle lessons and boundaries is a rite of passage in and of itself. Even though Mount Airy held my roots, South Philly was my molding, for better and for worse. In West Philly, or North, stratification of the races could happen more easily; less interaction needed to take place in blocks less crowded, less blended. But off of the river, next to the ports, attracting both the crooks and hard hustlers and tireless workers alike, South Philadelphia was Philly in its purest form.

A paradoxical world full of dualities. One that I have always mirrored.

YOU ARE YOUR PEOPLE.
EMBRACE YOUR EDGE.

CHAPTER 6
FAMILY

EARNEST LUQMAAN, ELDEST SURVIVING RELATIVE

TARIQ COMES FROM GOOD STOCK.

I had two good parents, parents that you really don't see that much today. I never even really heard my mother use profanity. I remember a time where we got one bike between my brothers and me for Christmas, and I can't recall any "It's my turn to ride." It was a very peaceful upbringing. I was in the middle, born in '43. Tariq's father, Tommy, was the youngest, born in '47, then we had an older brother, Clifton, born in 1941. And we all had our own style. We're brothers and all that, but we didn't travel together, we were just individuals and we respected each other.

Now, the oldest [Clifton] was more into the scholastic life, wants to go to college, wants to be in a fraternity. He ended up in the insurance business and had an office in Detroit. Once I visited Cliff in his office and saw a picture of the president on his wall. I look at the caption and it says, "Cliff, thank you for all of your advice." I said, "Cliff, you gave advice to the president?!" And he said, "No, man. I wrote that!" So, that's the way he was. And he liked living up on a hill. He liked that type of life. I went out there one time and they were barbecuing lobster tails. And I'm sitting outside, and he said, "Help yourself! I'm eating more lobster than I ever had in my life," and I said, "I ain't never had no such lobster!" And, I mean, that's what he liked to do. It was his style.

But everyone loved Tariq's father. He had the swagger, the looks, and I didn't realize how deep he was till I came back from the service. He was very logical. When I came back, I'm a Christian and all that, unmaimed, just floating. He had [become] a Black Muslim and told me, "Man, you should come this way." The logic and the persuasiveness were there. But I remember when he invited me I had a jar of pickled pig feet, and I said, "Yeah. As soon as I finish this pig's feet!" He said, "Now, if you come this way, you're going to have to get up in the morning and pray." I said, "How many times?" He said, "The rest of your life." That's what stuck to me. That's when I really started.

We were in the Nation of Islam and the Nation was pulling in people who were . . . streetwise. So, you can't avoid that. And Tommy became . . . well, he was respected and becoming, with his understanding and his knowledge, someone to reckon with. And he was good-looking. [At least] the women, they thought he was good. When you get like that, you have folks who don't like to see you in that position. He had enemies and that's pretty much what happened to him. But he was such a good person. He was a loved person and he was a rough person, but it was a good rough.

There's some things Tariq wanted to know from me about his [father's] demise. I told him it was because Tommy had the same character Tariq has—he was blessed with excellence and his excellence wasn't rehearsed. It was natural. And because of that, there was envy and jealousy. Malcolm [X] had that. People trying to hold him back because they're afraid he's going to outshine them. That's what happened. I'm talking on another cloud because those who know can understand what I'm saying.

Tommy's funeral was the biggest I've ever been to in my life. The streets off Susquehanna Ave were filled with so many people that, at the end, I remember the [police] captain came to me and he said, "Earnest, make an announcement and tell the people to go to their cars." So many people came to the wake. Cassandra was left with the two boys, Tariq and Keith. Tommy loved [Keith] just like he loved Tariq. I didn't see no difference. And he was more concerned because [Keith] had a little devilish in him at that time. You know how some of us do. [Tommy] said, "Now, Tariq's going to be right, but I got to get this one straight."

Cassandra was a very strong person. We had X's then—I was Earnest 12X and she had her X and all, and she was a lieutenant. So, at one point they said, "All the lieutenants go to Chicago and we're going to get rid of the X and give you a name." So, she went to Chicago. She came back and I said, "Cassandra, what name did they give you?" She said Luqmaan. I said—me flexing—"I'm going to accept that name for the whole family." Then I looked up the name and Luqmaan was a wise brother who would give advice, especially to the children, on how to respect their parents. The 31st surah of the Koran is titled Luqmaan the Wise. So, I love the name. I think it was 1987; I went to the court and legally changed my name from Trotter to Luqmaan. And I knew that I was going to make the Hajj, which I did in 1991. It was tremendous. The name Trotter is a reference to pig feet—they used to call pig feet "trotters." And I wasn't going over there with the name Earnest Pig Feet!

—

I REMEMBER MY FAMILY MEMBERS—aunts, cousins, uncles, and others—as figures with sharp outlines that my child's mind filled in with myths, intuition, overheard half-truths. As I grew older, the truth only got murkier the more I looked for it, and time only brought the erasure of whole swaths of relatives who could've shed light. Drugs. Violent deaths. Prison. But even in my fog of understanding, some things were clear: They were human. Emotional. Survivors whose lives depended on them learning fast. Hustlers in a city that forced you to move quick.

Ours was a bond that was unbreakable. We showed care through a willingness to spill blood for one another, secure bail, house and feed children, all while practicing forgiveness and nonjudgment over and over and over again. Both my paternal and maternal legacies were strong; theirs was a love willing to cut through any and all canyons of chaotic consequences to provide protection to their own. The level of their care flowed high and deep, like the runoff from the mountaintop that creates fresh spring rivers.

My paternal uncle Earnest Luqmaan is one of those family members who did not play. Uncle Luqmaan was in the organization with my father and had, according to legend, "done some things." He's an old-school elder statesman in the Muslim community and an organizer for veterans and their rights. But that man is a gangster who ran with a group that, when they were young, were allegedly very unassuming killers. I intentionally kept him at arm's length for a while. I remember when The Roots, then The Square Roots, first started rocking with our manager Rich Nichols, who passed in 2014. We were doing shows in the area and abroad, we had a record deal of some kind, but we weren't really making money. And Luqmaan didn't understand how we were not making money. I was young, trying to explain to him how the record industry works and how much it costs to do records and that we have to pay to tour and what all the overhead was, and he wasn't trying to hear none of that because he was like:

"The manager's this guy Rich, right?"

"Yeah."

"Rich Nichols? I mean . . . we can talk to him."

Silence.

"Shit, what?! I see you. We're *not* on the same page. You want to do *what* to my manager?! No."

MY FAMILY WAS PROTECTIVE OF THEIR TRIBE. I witnessed violence growing up, saw it firsthand even, but I was never in the trenches with the Grim Reaper picking souls for the other end of a bullet, the way numerous predecessors of my bloodline were. I grew up feeling like I was part of something—something that extended just outside my reach and view—that was intentionally hidden from me for my own good. I think my mother and my grandparents, my father's brothers, every one of my family members, did everything within their power to keep me from ending up executed in my twenties like my father. And then there was my half-brother, countless cousins, other people in my family who had been in and out of the prison system their whole lives who would also be held up as the shining example of a destiny to avoid: "Don't do what this motherfucker did. Whatever you do, please don't wind up like Keith. Please don't follow your cousins. Please don't do this . . . Please don't wind up like . . . You know what happened to your father, right?"

I didn't. Even that was kept hidden from me: growing up, I never fully knew what happened to him. Shit, I still don't know. As a child I worked to piece my father's murder together from reading newspaper clippings at my paternal grandparents' house. I'd be looking through the books in my grandmother's study and find some photos and old articles from the time around the investigation that told me more than anyone around me was willing to say. That's how I learned that the murder was an outright execution that was never solved. My father's brothers would give me little glimmers and bits of information. But no one ever told me, outright, what happened, as if telling the story would be like saying "Candyman" in the mirror three times and summoning this murder-mayhem dude to come forth and be after your ass. So, I was always playing detective and am *still* asking questions, trying to piece together the clues. Recent conversations with Uncle Luqmaan have finally given me some closure, but he'll likely take the fully colored-in and detailed truth with him to the grave.

The legacy on my maternal side was even more dense and complex, but less mysterious because I spent so much more time with them. My grandmother Minnie had three brothers: one was a gangster, one was a pimp, and one was a preacher. Her sisters were my great-aunts: Aunt Elanor, Aunt Viv, Aunt Dot, and Aunt Blanche, the latter nicknamed "Crazy Horse" for a reason I never learned. Aunt Blanche's husband was called "Pistol," and my grandmother? "Spike," although the way she told it, she got the name because she was always spiking drinks and could hook up a good punch. The streets said otherwise: I heard growing up that she, too, had a bit of a violent past and used to rock with an ice pick. I sometimes suspected that she had wielded one of the railroad spikes we used to play with from the train tracks about five blocks away at some encroaching man who underestimated her.

Alfonzo was the gangster. We called him Fonz, or Reds because he was a redbone dude, light-skinned with reddish brown hair. Uncle Reds was technically a retired gangster but still connected into that world. People would call Uncle Reds whenever there was trouble; if you needed somebody to get beat up or someone to bail you out, he was the one. Reds also always worked for the city, so he had a little bit of money and a house. Sometimes he would have to put his house up to get one of his boys out of jail, maybe somebody that he owed a debt to, who might have saved Reds's life back in the day from a dude who was going to slash his throat. Reds knew the code: if the man who saved you from a knife to the neck gets locked up, you put your house up and on the line for him.

Now, God forbid it was at the point of no return, you would call Uncle Willie. Willie was my grandmother's brother who was a pimp *and* a gangster, but he *wasn't* retired. Willie was still actively about that life. He had two sons who were also gangsters, both prominent JBM (Junior Black Mafia) drug lords in South Philly, making a lot of money and shooting up a lot of people. Both of Willie's sons were killed together when they were around twenty, ambushed and shot near City Hall while coming back from some touring comedy show.

And then there was Minnie's last brother, Uncle Bob. Bob Goldsmith was a preacher and his son, Robert Goldsmith, Jr., is a preacher. He probably has a son named Robert who is *also* a preacher. Uncle Bob was the Martin Luther King of the family, and there's not much to say about him except that maybe his prayers helped us all. Unclear.

So, when it came to undoing or handling something, the general consensus was that if Fonzo can't straighten it out, then maybe Willie could fix it. But if it was some sincere next-level request that was both out of anybody's hands and above everybody's heads, then you could call Uncle Willie's sons' cousin on their mother's side, who was about that life too. Living only half a block away from me on the same street as my grandmother, this third cousin was a big drug dude in South Philly and also a genuinely sweet, kind person. One day he was kidnapped and held for ransom, and once his kidnappers got the money, they still killed him and put him in a dumpster.

The women held their own, with a particular brand of warrior-like toughness born out of the times that confronted them. My great-aunt Vivian, Shawn's mom, was completely deaf, having lost her hearing when she was a child or adolescent. Hearing impairment on my mother's side of the family was common among the women. My grandmother was hard of hearing, my grandmother's sister Dot was also very hard of hearing, and Dot had two completely deaf daughters. Aunt Viv herself had another completely deaf and mute child, one of Shawn's brothers. So, we were always around hearing impairment and I grew up accustomed to it. What was different about Aunt Viv is that if she didn't tell you she was deaf, you would have no clue. She was super sharp in her understanding: reading the room, energy, lips. Aunt Viv was like a Black Sophia Loren, with the big sunglasses, hair always done, nails always painted, fly coats and shoes and all that. That might be one of the things that made her one of my favorite aunts. I just thought, "Yo, this lady's fly. And I respect fly people." And Aunt Viv didn't take any shit. She raised her four children very sternly. My Uncle Eddie G, her husband, was a prison guard and a correctional officer at Holmesburg Prison in Northeast Philly, and they got into real estate pretty early on. Aunt Viv and Eddie G had multiple properties in the city, including that house on Sharpnack Street we once called home.

MY MOTHER'S FIRST SON, Keith, and I don't have the same father. His father is this guy named George from South Philly who was a big real estate dude and a fireman. I would see George all the time around the way and I knew his other sons. I always liked George, but Keith didn't associate with that whole side of the family. When I went to Millersville University for a year, one of my best friends was a girl named Augustine, who we all called Coco. She and I called each other brother and sister because of how close we were. But in a crazy coincidence, Coco is actually my half-brother's half-sister. Wild. When I would come home from school, I would spend whatever time we had off at George's house with his family, which was on the other side of South Philly. My half-brother used to be mad as hell about the fact that I had that relationship with his actual brothers and sisters. Keith was quick to tell me, "Them niggas don't love you."

South Philly held the contradictions that would shape me: There was deep love, expressed by a family who somehow knew the importance of insulating me from the full scale of deeds that were only insinuated. And there was the hardness found on those same small blocks, whose message was exactly what Keith believed: *Them niggas don't love you.* My family, my mother, the men she dated, everyone that I grew up with and around in South Philly sang their dystopian hymn with a united voice: *Shit might look sweet, but don't get it fucked up.* And it was the lessons of living on that edge, that constant teetering on the fine line between cool and crazy, that embedded themselves deep into my psyche in those years after the bliss of a life uptown in Mount Airy. They are layered in me now.

SOMETIMES TO
GET HOME YOU'VE GOT TO
GET ON DOWN THE ROAD.

CHAPTER 7
BALTIMORE

IN THE SUMMER OF MY TWELFTH YEAR MY MOTHER DE-cided to sell what we could sell and pack what we could pack and move to Baltimore. She and I left town with one of her sisters in the faith, my Aunt Naima.

BALTIMORE DIDN'T LAST VERY LONG.

But I think her goal was to just get us out of Philly, and in retrospect I'm sure it had something to do with criminality or drugs. We sold her coveted console and couch, the last remnants of the first floor of our old home. I sold some art I'd made and some of my personal belongings so that I had a couple dollars in my pocket. It felt like an adventure. A pickup truck came to grab what was left, everything we had dragged out to the sidewalk, and we loaded up, got in the back, and set off. For whatever reason, we wound up having to leave the truck and take the bus. I remember sitting at the bus station, still excited.

For some other mysterious reason, though, we went to Washington, D.C., first. In D.C. we still had a little money, but we were being selective about what we paid for and what we scammed. We stayed at hotels and then dipped, running up a few days' worth of bills, hopping from one place to the next before they caught on. By the time we left D.C. for Baltimore, in the peak of the summer season, everything was a scam. We were away from family and friends, and money was tight: *You want snacks, you want toys or coloring books, you want anything? Go out in the streets and get it.* We'd steal magic sets, disappearing ink, cards, or whatever we needed and wanted to help make the time pass. As the seasons started to change and it got a little colder, things got harder. We were just completely fucked up. We were going to the government assistance offices in Baltimore to get free groceries and living in a motel on the north side, eating tiny cans of mackerel. At one point, I don't remember who it was, but probably Aunt Naima, said, "This is some bullshit. Let's at least send the kid back to Philly." So my mom and I took the train back to Philly, where she left me to stay with Minnie.

It didn't seem like my mom was unraveling. It seemed like the adults had a plan, at least at first. And I wouldn't have dared question her. There was no "Why are we doing this?" because the answer would have been "'Cause I fucking said so." When we got to Philly, Minnie thought it best for us both to be closer to her for a while. So while I lived with Minnie, my mom got her own apartment on the same block. I moved back in with my mom full-time for a little bit and went back to school. But that was short-lived. After a couple months my mom needed to get away from her mother again. While I stayed with Minnie, Mom moved into some projects in a different part of South Philly, shacked up with one of her boyfriends.

My grandmother knew her only child: Cassie was stubborn, and no one could impose their will on her or convince her to do anything that she didn't want to do. And it was clear at this time that Mom was becoming addicted to the street life. But Minnie had a vision for my half-brother and me, her only grandkids, and believed that if you want something done right, you have to do it yourself. By the time I moved in, Keith was already living with her because of the constant fighting that he and my mother got into. I don't know if my grandmother saw all that was coming with my mom, but I'm sure she knew that it was time for her to intervene.

A GRANDMOTHER'S PRAYERS

CHAPTER 8
MINNIE

IF MY MOTHER WAS THE HEART OF MY LIFE, WHOSE UNconditional love animated my rhythms year after year, then Minnie was its soul, the expansive spirit that inhabited the best part of me, even after her pulse stopped. Minnie lived at South 5th and McKean Streets, along with her second husband, Leemore Everett, who I knew as Grandpa. The Mother Teresa of the neighborhood, she embodied the proverbial "It takes a village," putting the concept of family and community first. Minnie was the wise sage, church elder, and matron saint, by nature and by profession: she worked for the Mayor's Office of Community Services. She was who we all turned to in times of celebration and struggle. She knew the intimate histories of everyone on the block, was called "Mom" by all, and was deeply invested in the neighborhood that housed her entire family. I officially moved in with Minnie when I was twelve, but in some sense I always lived with her. In the summertime and on weekends my mother was moving and grooving, liable at any time to blurt out, "I'm about to drop you off at Minnie's," with no objections from me.

My grandmother and her siblings had originally come to

Philly from Greenville, South Carolina, as children, settling in South Philly into a set of tightly compact row homes within a five-block radius. Being at her home thus granted me access to my cousins, aunts, uncles, and their stories. For most of my childhood their small brick homes sat squatly on cobblestone streets, the rounded and uneven gray stones typical of Philly's original neighborhoods. Later, the city would pull up all the charm of those roads, opting to restrict cobblestone to the historic districts like Old City, near Independence Hall, and paving our streets in dull and slick black-tar asphalt.

Minnie's was a humble contemporary three-bedroom, in which I had my own room. My grandparents took pride in their home. She and my grandfather kept the décor on par with whatever was *en vogue* at the time; brown textural wood panels of the '70s transitioned to the reflective silver mirrors of the '80s, their ceiling going from dropped to popcorn-textured to match the aesthetics—like, who does that? *Cool, we can afford to drop the ceiling, we want less space!* Earth-tone shag carpets protected the floors from the tread of heavy footfalls with their textures, in turn, guarded by softly crunching thin plastic runners. Zippered vinyl covers that never really softened to our body heat kept dirt and dyes and grime off the gold-colored sofa and matching loveseat. The whole scene was anchored by the unchanging glass-and-brass décor of the coffee and side tables with built-in attached lamps. My grandfather's La-Z-Boy recliner sat turned towards the color TV, whose presence marked the boundary between the entry vestibule and the sitting area. Like typical row homes in Philly, the whole first-floor living area was "open-concept" well before the style became the design buzzword of the 2010s. The window in the room was mounted with an AC unit that we were only allowed to use in the dead of summer, and even then only if it was above a hundred degrees and we had company. The small backyard never reached its full potential; more than anything it was a place for us to hang laundry out to dry. And the basement was unfinished, but we still gathered there: generations of grandchildren, children, aunts, and sisters, congregating together under the safety of Minnie's roof.

The house was fronted by a decorative wrought-iron gate, which created a small porch out front, something that most people on the block absolutely could not afford. But Minnie and her sister Blanche could: if there were maybe five houses with the gates, hers and Aunt Blanche's were two of them. That, plus some aluminum siding to the front façade, made the house stand out, fresh amidst the typical red brick of the South Philly neighborhood.

My grandparents had one of the best houses on the block, but they were still intensely private—both of them came from the school of "We ain't even turning the indoor lights on at nighttime unless the blinds and curtains are drawn." And while that gate was decorative, it was also functional. They knew it was crazy out there. We lived in the middle of a wild neighborhood with shooting and robbing and stealing, and nine times out of ten the one performing the violence was someone we grew up with, who lived right next door to us, or our cousins, or their kids. The gate was a useful ornament and a beautiful tool. No choice was made for one reason, no act was singular in its desired effect, no decoration could lack function. They did everything with intention.

Minnie's first husband, my mother's father, was named Howard Bowen, but I knew him as Howie. Howie was not as G as my grandmother, but he was chill. After they split up, Minnie didn't really fuck with Howie like that, and my mom didn't either. But he was good with me. Sometimes on a Sunday, Howie would come pick me up and I would ride in the back of his car, listening to the oldies, doo-wop and Butterball-type Harvey Holiday stuff, heading to hang out at his crib in the Oak Lane/Cheltenham area.

My grandmother's second husband, my grandpa, was named Leemore and had an identical twin brother named Leroy. Both were just cool motherfuckers: old school, pencil-thin mustache, the Donny Hathaway–style hat. Anyone that I ever looked up to was about that brim life. Leemore had a steel wardrobe in the bedroom where he would keep additional clothes, and on top of it sat stacks and stacks of hat boxes, from summer joints to brim hats, fedoras, flat caps, and newsboys. He reminded me of Fred Flintstone, this manly man who was also a gentle giant, whistling all the time, singing little songs, and scatting as he walked around the house. He was very much a provider and enjoyed that identity—the whole idea and feeling of "bringing home the bacon." Returning home from getting the groceries, he would beam with a certain satisfaction as we met him at the curb to bring the plastic and paper bags into the house, like, *Yeah. I brought the food home yet again. We're hunter-gatherers out this bitch.*

He was also a hustler. Leemore drove a meat truck for the Italians, like Robert De Niro in the Scorsese flick *The Irishman,* which was also shot in that neighborhood. My grandpa was as close to an old Italian as an old Black man could be. He was involved in some kind of criminal activity with that meat truck. They must have paid him in cash because he always kept a brick of money in his pocket and in his wallet. I would dip into that wad, swearing he was clueless.

But of course he knew. Faith in that same fallacy gave me the gall to also take his cars for joyrides when I was twelve, thirteen years old. Leemore stayed with a pimped-out ride:

his first car was a sleek and shiny, long-ass black Lincoln Continental whose gray steering wheel I could hardly see over, followed by a dark green Buick Regal with a ragtop. I would watch my half-brother taking the car and bringing it back to the exact same parking spot with Leemore seemingly none the wiser, but Keith was seven or eight years older than me and slicker with it. That didn't matter to me, though—I wanted to do the same thing. For a while I thought I was getting away with it. But all it took was one night to blow the illusion.

Leemore used to take day trips to Atlantic City via Greyhound bus or with friends, and one day while he was out, I took his car for a ride with the goal of parking it before he returned from the casino. Atlantic City is an hour away and the trips would see him back well into the evening, so I thought I would be fine. But when it was time to bring the car back to its original parking spot, another driver had taken the space. I had to wait for that person to eventually move their car, knowing that the key to pulling this off was parking in precisely the same location. But as I waited for this irksome person to return, someone who Leemore had probably asked to keep an eye on his car noticed that it wasn't there—unbeknownst to me. Once the spot finally freed up, I reverted back to the original plan, parked his car (as best I could then), and then called myself sneaking back in the crib. But when I walked through the door Leemore was already home, waiting and ready. He hit me dead in my chest and knocked the wind out of me just as I was stepping past the threshold of the front hallway. I fell backwards onto the floor, a bit stunned. After a moment or two down there, I collected myself, and as I got back up he very simply said, "Give me the keys." He was sharp enough to know that I must have had a set of keys made (my half-brother did this too, so we never had to go in Leemore's pocket and steal them outright). I handed them over and that ended the charade. It was the only time he ever put his hands on me.

The cars of that era—those owned by Leemore, or Howie, or even my Uncle Pistol—carried the specific scent of unfiltered tobacco blending with the oiled smell of real leather. The feeling of sitting in the backseat with the city rolling past while these grown men smoked their cigars or cigarettes, the husky burnt leaves accented by the deep, bright undertone of fresh leather, was engrained into my being. It's a scent that's deeply nostalgic, a portal to memories of men I admired. Even now when I'm shopping for a fragrance to wear or a candle, I gravitate towards tobacco and leather or wood. It is a comfort.

Growing up in Minnie's house had me under the impression that it was normal for kids to all pull their weight and to pay their own way. I would ask her for money and she would respond, "Here's three dollars, you need to eat, but don't expect this from me all the time. You need to get out there and see who needs help with something. See who's hiring and see where you could get a job." No handouts. It runs in my blood to be a hustler, but Minnie was above the board with her connections: she knew of all the government summer programs, random neighborhood job opportunities, and various other options for me to explore and take advantage of. Whether it was city hall or the local neighborhood store, she was always willing to put in a good word.

Even before I lived with them, I respected how hard Minnie and Leemore worked to provide for our family and beyond. But over time I gained a deeper appreciation for the interior rhythm of their lives. The crazier my life outside of the home became, the more I loved and needed the grounding peacefulness of their routines (even if I had to hide a knife or a gun before I walked in, or if I entered their home in a heart-racing sweat, after running blocks to get away from something or someone). The fluidity of their lifestyle was engrained in every corner of the house, a current on which I willingly flowed. That deeper appreciation started when I first found myself living there at twelve.

When Minnie would get off the bus coming home from work I was always excited, waiting at the screen door for her arrival, watching her walk the two short blocks from the bus stop, stopping here and there to chat with or greet people, maybe pop into the little corner store to play the numbers, before leisurely making her way to our house. Upon entering the crib, she would find me ready to unlace her boots, helping her get them off by pulling on their short stout heels. I loved the comfort of sitting up close to her when she was on that vinyl-covered velvet sofa. Lying at her feet felt natural, like sanctuary, so close that I could feel them still throbbing from her workday. I never felt as safe as I did during those times. As the evening approached, she'd finally recline, maybe getting on the phone, or we'd watch *Wheel of Fortune* or the six o'clock news, me sitting next to her or at the foot of my grandfather's La-Z-Boy. Waiting patiently for their programs to end so that I could change the channel.

Leemore would die in this home on Easter Sunday in the late eighties. I had spent the morning in church with my grandmother and then linked up with my girlfriend at the time, heading ten blocks north to her house after services to cook chicken cutlets. It was sunny and warm, everyone was outside. I was wearing a cherry-red-and-gray Adidas sweatsuit and some clean black Air Force 1s, Easter fresh. It was nighttime by the time I got back, and Leemore was reclining in the living room watching *Jeopardy*. Per usual, I sat at his feet in quiet communion. He eventually decided to go upstairs, cheerfully singing his usual scats and *ba-da-doop deeeeeee dum,* humming melodies—damn near like a sitcom character—when all of a sudden his breathing changed, becoming more and more labored as he struggled to climb up the stairs, only to collapse at the top. We called 911, and EMTs came and tried to tend to him in my grandparents' bedroom, while Minnie and I looked on in shock. They had to take him to the hospital, but he was a really large man, so trying to get him back down the stairs of this tight South Philly row home was challenging. Once they finally did, we went to the hospital, Minnie riding inside the ambulance with him, me close behind in the car with his daughter. But Leemore was pronounced dead on arrival. There would forever be a void in that home. Though my grandmother lived for family and for community, her husband always came first. After his passing, something shifted in her.

At Minnie's, I learned of the beauty of true intimacy—what love could look like when all pretense disintegrated into truth. The joy of mutuality. Learning to care for someone in their own language, acts of love as natural and consistent and calm as breathing. Love was the essence, the basis of every action, and profound beauty flowed from this commitment. I knew the challenges of the world were real and chaotic and the streets were deadly and tempting, but in their home Minnie and Leemore showed me that an alternate universe of intention and care existed: chosen, built, lived in. Reciprocity so strong that it bound a family and a community: still, deep, and steady. On South 5th Street the banal became art, elevated by a loyal love.

FOR MY WHOLE LIFE I've been chasing the soulfulness of their partnership and the tranquility of their lives, hoping to re-create and root myself in that same feeling. I wanted what they had: to lead a family and reliably support a home life. It hasn't been a straight road for me. I've struggled with that responsibility in ways that more closely mirrored my mother: addiction, in my case to weed and liquor, tinting the clarity and disrupting the consistency that would allow me to embody the role full-time. With my older children, I wasn't ready or present enough, considering the point I was at in my life and career. But with my marriage and the birth of my daughter and then my youngest son, I worked harder to be like the elders I admired for those under my care. In my wife I felt like I found the foundational partnership for that ideal of home. We're committed to that vision, choosing home and family, even when it's hard for us to choose each other. The importance and power of home is not just about a building, it's about having a space for love and self and family to be fully expressed, which becomes a beacon for the wider circle of friends and family to gather, sit down, and be loved. The home I'm trying to create now is the far-off echo of a period in my early life when I fully accepted care. An homage to that sanctuary on the 1900 block of South 5th Street and all of the grace and peace that Minnie bestowed on her lineage and tribe, and especially on me.

HOLD ON TO YOUR PEOPLE.

CHAPTER 9
IT TAKES A VILLAGE

THE ESSENCE OF MINNIE'S PHILOSOPHY WAS COMMU-nity. As a community organizer, she knew the importance of the village coming together to upkeep and uplift the neighborhood, and, more important, to raise its children. Minnie instilled that same value in my mother, who surrounded me with her family, blood and chosen: her girlfriends and her brothers and sisters in Islam, figures whose strength and light supported her own.

Within my mother's tribe, there was my Aunt Naima, who went by a lot of different names: Naima Bey, Naima Beyah, Barbara Boyd, Barbara Bey. But to me, she was simply my Aunt Na. Her willingness to ride out with my mother for our brief stint in Baltimore was evidence of her love and respect for Cassie. The two were both high-ranking female lieutenants in the Nation of Islam at that time, willing to pray together or fuck bitches up. Aunt Na had three sons and one daughter—respectively Hammed, Faheem, Kareem, and Kimyatta, who we called Kim—and dated a brother named El, who was like an uncle to me. They all lived relatively close by, in fact only a block over from young Beanie Sigel, the rapper, who I knew growing up.

El was a tailor (whether he worked in some dry cleaner somewhere or some tailor shop, I don't know) and the reason I missed my tenth birthday party. He made pants for Aunt Na's sons that I consistently complimented and loved, so when my birthday was about to roll around he promised to make me some pants for the big day. It was my first custom pair—freshly made gabardine navy blue slacks, they were *crazy*—and I spent the morning of waiting for them to come straight off the sewing machine, hot off the ironing board. I knew how to gauge quality even then; we were all about that fly life: me and Aunt Na's boys were always fresh because our parents were credit card and check scammers—and when the stores didn't have what we needed, we could get what we wanted via mail-order catalog fraud or buying from boosters. And my mom had dated tailors in the past, so my sense of style was already next-level.

When El said he was making me these pants for my birthday, I got some white-on-white Nike blazers so I was ready to show up at my party with custom navy blue pants and shiny white sneaks on. But listen . . . El miscalculated his work time that day, and I refused to go to the party without my pants, so I just waited till he was done. He didn't finish the pants till six or seven in the evening, but we had invited everyone over for a start time of maybe one in the afternoon. When I finally got to the crib to celebrate, all my friends had come and gone. Anticlimactic. But I looked fly as shit.

While my mother found Aunt Na and her peoples in our Muslim community, my grandmother's tribe was the Christianity. Her rootedness in the church meant that I grew up there too, by her side at Phillip Temple Christian Methodist Church at South 3rd and Fitzwater. My mother was fine with me attending church activities to keep from being idle, so long as I didn't get "spooked"—which to her meant eating swine or coming home baptized ("Don't let anybody put that water on you!"). I was never baptized, sworn in, or signed up to the Christian life, but they used to take trips and had cake and food and talent shows, and I went. I wanted to have fun with kids my own age, even though hanging with these Christians was a bit like living a double life.

Church was also a way to dive deeper into my creativity. My family recognized from a young age that I was a performer. At church I joined the choir, met other singers, and joined smaller performance groups, which eventually led my grandmother and mother to get me into a youth chorus for people from our neighborhood.

The church also had its elders who would become my own. Arthur Price was a young man, close to me in age, but he was serious and highly respected by adults even when he was only a teenager himself. His deep patience and compassionate, peaceful spirit resonated with me. Given the title "youth advisor," Arthur was also the grandson of the other Minnie—Minnie Davis—and the nephew of James Black, the man my mother dated for a while, so he felt like family. We all knew that Arthur was going to be a preacher—and in fact, he's now the pastor of 16th Street Baptist in Birmingham, Alabama. I would turn to him regularly at pivotal moments in my life. He was a mentor and key figure in helping me cope with the lingering feelings of grief and loss that haunted me.

But I would learn and absorb just as much from the men on the corners, hood griots willing to share their tales with the deserving, their watchful eyes roaming the block. I would synthesize wisdom from the men in the barbershops, a community watering well that overflowed with information. These small rooms had their own hustle, I discovered. You could sell your seat to the anxious and impatient who came in hoping to be squeezed in or were pressed for time to leave. They'd walk into a full shop and, surveying the line of folks waiting for their barber, offer to pay someone who was closer to the chair for their spot. As I moved up the waiting list I'd let folks pay one, two, maybe even three times for my place, willing to sit in the shop all day to absorb all that was poured forth while getting the twenty dollars needed for my haircut and then some. Even when I had locs. I cut them just to get back to the environment of the shop.

We didn't have much, but we knew the importance of leaning on each other. I was curious as a kid, smart enough to know that asking adults directly for advice or information would lead to skewed answers based on what they wanted me to hear or the limits of their own experience. But if I could observe and see what was said and left unsaid—the meaning conveyed in the lifting of an eyebrow, the modulation of tone, the shifting of shoulders, even what was admitted in a soft voice when no one thought I was paying close attention—then I could learn the truth. My introversion became a new vantage point, a sharper lens allowing me to see the deeper layers of the worlds around me. The revelations of one soul coloring in the mysteries of another.

AND THEN THERE WERE MY FRIENDS. Ours was a wartime bond. From scaling walls to tag our names all over Philly, to watching crack hit the neighborhoods and destroy families, we went through it together. My grandmother spoke with a thousand proverbs: "A hard head make a soft behind." "Good manners will take you further in life than money ever will." "Don't flash your money in a crowd." One thing she said that I found laughable then but that came back to me as a curse was: "You're going to go through life and you'll be able to count your real friends on one hand."

"Man, you buggin," I would say. "I got like fifty friends! That's my man, that's my man, that's my man, she my homie."

And Minnie would look at me and say, "Yeah, those aren't your friends. You'll see. Just over time. Time will tell."

There was Hammed, the "cousin" that I was with that first fight night in South Philly, son of Aunt Na. After him were the two guys we got into it with outside of the corner store: Odell and Otis—two brothers. They would start what we called The Equal Team, T.E.T., with a bunch of other homies: Splash, who passed in 2019, the OG of the hood who everybody looked up to; and then Aaron, Dave, and Moose, with Charlie Kahn and Chaka coming into the picture once we got to high school. In our early days we would all cross South Philly to hang out at the railroad tracks, where the Conrail freight trains were routed over these small overpasses. Venturing down 25th Street and across damn near the whole of South, we'd arrive at "Cowboy" and "Cowgirl," two small, fat hills that the train tracks sat on, maybe twenty blocks apart. The train tracks were active. We'd go on them knowing that somebody got their leg or arm cut off while playing around and sneaking on the train tracks like us. But we didn't care. We threw "Jesus nails" at each other, the big-ass pure-iron heavy-as-hell spikes that held the train tracks in place and were, in our imaginations, the same brand of nail that pierced Jesus when he was crucified on the cross. You only needed to get hit with one of them one good time to know you better not get hit again. We would also have bottle fights, rock fights, and dirt bomb wars; flipping on pissy mattresses and break-dancing on the sidewalk all were natural, locally grown remedies for boredom.

We were like brothers. Eventually, a young man named Ahmir Thompson, who I would meet at CAPA, the city's art high school, would join this inner circle of real friends. The kind you could count on one hand.

BUT MINNIE WAS RIGHT—over time, all of my relationships have revealed themselves. There have been people I thought I would be friends with for life, people I've considered brothers or sisters, but who weren't who they had said they were and who fell by the wayside. My grandmother taught me the importance of surrounding yourself only with the people who have earned the right to be in your space, who have earned your trust, and earned your love, and earned the right to share in your joy. Our paths intertwine with so many people, but there's a meaningful gap between the real ones and those just passing through.

PART III

WHAT IS YOUR ART

A CULTURE BUILT THROUGH COMMUNITY

CHAPTER 10
WORLD OF HIP-HOP

IT'S HARD TO EXPLAIN TO PEOPLE WHO WEREN'T THERE what it was like to watch hip-hop and rap unfold like a new renaissance. Growing up on the sounds of the '60s and '70s, Black music accented by swinging and staccatos, we were primed for a shift in the way we heard melodies by artists like James Brown and Lionel Richie. Adding Jamaican DJ culture to our parties on the streets and in the parks, the emcee was born. A whole new rhythm was emerging from this intersection of shared sonic history, trickling down to us in Philly from New York. It came in fast-moving waves of innovation, experimentation, and invention as we grew from children to adolescents.

I studied the evolving art of the emcee record by record: listening to Grandmaster Flash and the Furious Five, the Treacherous Three; Grandmaster Caz showed me how a rap can take narrative form and an emcee can find new patterns and rhythms within a beat; Spoonie Gee and his track "Love Rap" further trained me how to paint a picture with words; and "The Micstro" by Radiänce had its fast-paced beat, live instrumentation, and rhymes by RC LaRock that were quick and sharp and inspiring as hell. Explicit, hypervisual narratives, playing with various flows and different pockets, these wordsmiths' version of jazz felt intimately familiar, an extension of my own family's record collections and stories. Finally, Rakim would be the one whose flow truly inspired my own.

With all this new music and language swirling around me, I did what I knew best and returned to books. This is when my favorite competitive cousin, Shawn Gee, and I started to pick random words from the dictionary and try to put them in the best four-to-eight-bar raps we could imagine. That simple exercise became my training ground. Tapping into books—even the dictionary—for inspiration was a habit that became core to not just how I write, but also how I think. Reading sparked my imagination in a way similar to art, catapulting me into worlds and concepts far beyond my immediate surroundings. The universe opened. It was greater than just Philadelphia, more nuanced and specific than the first- and secondhand knowledge that I had access to in my environment. As I grew as a person and as a performer, books would color my perspective and give my lyrics more depth than my peers'.

I wrote my first rap at nine years old and, as first songs are, it was an imitation of rhythms and flows I admired. But as I kept writing, my rhymes reflected how I was already taking it all in—not just the artists of note who were becoming famous in New York, but the unknown artists in Philly who could rap just as well. People off the block. People on the corners. As kids we would listen to all of it and then find ourselves at the center of this new world at neighborhood parties. At that time in Philly there was the constant flow of block parties, basement parties, parties in the park. If it was hot outside, which felt like damn near every day in the summer, me and my friends would find a party somewhere outside where we could be like flies on the wall, watching this world unfold. We may have been some of the youngest in the crowd, but it didn't raise a brow. Everybody would be out there. Adults, teens, little kids. The events were all-inclusive, and anybody was welcome to come and get down. That's what hip-hop was: something truly for us and by us. It spoke to us, as a people and a culture, a community, and even down to the level of individual blocks, written wholly in our distinct languages.

I formed my first band in fourth grade, a rap group called the Crash Crew. It was me, Hammed, Beanie Sigel, who was then in third grade, my man Randy on the beatbox, another rapper named Walik, and a couple of graffiti artists who made us T-shirts. I had competed in the school talent show the year before when I was in third grade, singing DeBarge's ballad "I Like It," and lost to somebody who was popping and locking on some hip-hop shit. After that, I turned to my friends and said, "Yeah, I'm not singing in the talent shows no more: next time I come back to this talent show, I'm rapping. Who's with me?" And so our little crew was formed.

The day finally comes and we're all excited about the show, wearing our T-shirts, and at some point in the day I start doing a human beatbox, posted in the corner of the lunchroom so I could get some extra bass from the closeness of the walls. The vice principal sees me and starts tripping, like, "That's obscene. What are you doing?!" And on the spot he suspended me for behaving obscenely. At that point, the human beatbox wasn't common and was hyperspecific to young people in the Black community, what was happening in the streets, a culture I'm sure he was clueless about. And here I am in the corner of the lunchroom making these *brummpp-PSH!* sounds seemingly to myself, bobbing my head and moving my body to this made-up beat and he's bug-eyed and disturbed, looking at me like, "Yo . . . what are you doing?! Get out of the corner. You are suspended, *and* I need to talk to your mom."

My mom was at work and there was no one to come and get me, so I was allowed to ride out the rest of the day. But they were clear: "You're suspended. You can't do the talent show." Did they just expect me to sit there in the audience while Beans and them were onstage? Come on. I had the shirt on and everything! So when I see the Crash Crew, my crew, walk onstage to perform, I got on the stage, too! The administrators are admonishing me to come down, but I did my rap. It was an unplanned speed rap—I had to rap that jawn fast as fuck because the vice principal was chasing me from one side of the stage to the other while I performed.

We won that talent show. I put together another rap group to compete in a church talent show, called the TMT Crew—Tyrone, Marcelus, and Tariq. And we would win that one too.

AS A GENRE AND EMERGING LIFESTYLE, hip-hop was softening the boundaries between local factions. Philly, as a whole, is small, and South Philly is even smaller, and our side of South was even smaller and divided by Washington Avenue, which was essentially the train tracks. People from our side of the tracks—this little eight-to-ten-block radius—didn't really fuck with the people (also Black) who were on the other side, often for some Hatfield/McCoydian reasons unknown. But every Sunday, we would go skating at this rink called St. Charles, on the other side of the tracks. Fighting our way through the hood to get there. And even if you made it to the rink and it was all good, by the time we were ready to go home, we would have to throw hands on the way back to get out of that neighborhood. But with hip-hop, if there was something going on in the park or on a block, the music became the common denominator and a unifying factor. You would see people letting their guard down, allowing folks who they normally beef with or get tense around pull up and partake like it was a family affair. Moments like this were always happening. We would go to a recreation center called The Center on 7th and Snyder that also had a public swimming pool, swings and sliding board, monkey bars over concrete that would absolutely fuck up your knees if you fell, and basketball courts. My friends and I would climb to the rooftop of the building and look down on the jams and the parties happening below. Before we had enough confidence to try and grab the mic, we just sat and observed, soaking it all in.

Hip-hop brought a level of escapism with it. This was the Reagan era, the very beginnings of crack's infiltration. The realities of all these places we lived, big inner cities, were so harsh that folks were looking for something, anything, to be that outlet of freedom. And hip-hop was there for it. A way to laugh to keep from crying. It's damn near a common principle between Black and Brown people on this earth: when you look at indigenous villages that have been slaughtered or colonized beyond recognition, you can witness whoever is still holding on to whatever is still left engaging in their traditional festivities, still celebrating life, their heritage, their culture, their universe. We see indigenous communities around the world dedicated to upholding their ceremonies and languages and dances. It's not just a matter of maintaining their history despite all that they've faced—these musical movements also give them a way of seeing and taking care of themselves; in spite of whatever grief that has come to them, their desire to dance and feed their souls is unbroken. That's what hip-hop was for us.

—

AND IT JUST KEPT EVOLVING. With Afrika Bambaataa & Soulsonic Force's "Planet Rock" came an entirely new rhythm that damn near possessed the streets: all of a sudden people knew every word, cried out over the beat, moved differently with a new style of sharp staccato dance movements. Watching it wash over us in all its cultural glory solidified in me that hip-hop was it. "Planet Rock" hooked me. It was the first record I ever bought—even the Tommy Boy logo was mesmerizing to me, a silhouette of people dancing, one of the dancers a B-boy spinning on his head. It all seemed so new. "Planet Rock" was my true gateway drug.

Afrika Bambaataa dressed like a shaman, but when Run-DMC came on the scene with their series of big hits in the early '80s, for the first time I saw hip-hop that looked familiar, rappers who could've been corner boys or other people I knew in Philly. Gone was the vibe of R&B singers, punk rockers, or funk singers. Sweat suits and sneakers and fedoras and leather were in. Rappers were now more familiar and became the definition of cool.

The seismic shift wasn't just in the streets. There was a youthful rebellion boiling over with hip-hop films that captured and spread the DNA of that era: *Breakin', Krush Groove, Wild Style,* and *Beat Street*. Anarchist undertones and lead actors close to my age made me want to emulate this new visual inspiration, tropes simultaneously reinforced by emerging street art documentaries and magazines. Amidst all of this I started writing graffiti more seriously—"Double T" was my name and mark. Textbooks and folders with homework assignments were replaced by black marbled notebooks and cans of paint in our backpacks for us to perfect our designs before canvassing the city or waiting expectantly to run into other graff artists to exchange sketchbooks: *Maybe I'll do something in your book, you'll do something in mine.* A method of artistic collaboration and cooperation. Once the visions were written down, we took those ideas to the larger canvases of the city: a train, a wall, or the white side of a truck. It upped the ante of my old creative competition with Shawn: I was still competing but with larger goals and a small crew that demanded courage and execution. We were parkour artists, running around the city from West Philly's 69th Street to the Northeast, scaling walls and fences, and jogging through subterranean tunnels, teetering on wooden planks across alleyways to venture, undetected, from roof to roof. To reach the most insane places to show off the talents of every writer we ran with.

My mother would think I was just hanging out in the neighborhood, but all of Philadelphia had become my playground. Rooting myself deeper in a creative life felt liberating. It allowed me to build on the expansiveness of reading books but also made me crave a life that was just outside of my grasp. I loved the way we could find expression in any creative outlet, moving fluidly between disciplines and growing in skill—that versatility became a cornerstone of my identity as an artist, and lives on in the various interests I've cultivated since. I never saw the world as black or white, never felt that any one art form should dominate another. No, we *had* to do it all. The boundaries always blurred, culture was never just one thing, and if you were doing it right, a movement could be limitless. We were those young people on the screen, the oldheads in the park, the cool corner boys, the unseen faces behind the city's tags. We drew from the best of all these worlds, existing in their intersections, as we let every ounce of expression run through us.

THE STREET'S ART CLASSES

CHAPTER 11
GRAFFITI

GRAFFITI FOR ME WAS JUST ANOTHER HAND. I HAD BEEN working on creative styles and scripts for as long as I had been able to write. By the time I was nine, graffiti was everywhere in Philly, etched on walls, doors, buses, benches. A whole generation was hell-bent on making sure its presence was felt and remembered. We were always practicing—it was important that you knew your signature imprint inside and out so that when a canvas presented itself, you were ready. Black notebooks became battlegrounds for ideas to emerge. *Write, write, write, write, write.* If I wasn't practicing my tag, then I was doing pieces—more colorful, elaborate mural-like ideas but on a smaller scale—or graffiti men, as we would call them. They were different characters, cool-looking figures that might have an oversized box cut and be holding a boom box or posted up in a B-boy stance.

The T.E.T. crew got into graffiti writing. Aaron, who would tag "She-Rock," would stick with it for life. Hammed still writes. Dave's tag was "Saran" and Charlie's was "Cee." And I was right there with them. We went from playing on the railroad track to finding abandoned houses—"bandos"—to tag. We would tunnel into basements and scale the walls of abandoned buildings filled with dead dogs and trash to practice. I didn't do big murals, but Hammed and Aaron would. They got further along in the graffiti world than me, due to a twist of fate.

At that time in Philly, every graffiti writer, anyone from any crew who was active and worth their salt, would go to a meeting every couple weeks on the roof of this glass factory. It was a town hall for graffiti writers to gather, offer up their grievances, and address beefs. There would be anything from ten to twenty people in the room, and we were the youngest kids that would attend, still just ten or eleven years old. So folks started to know us because we were all over the city tagging. One time, some of us were down by the 30th Street Station train tracks where there was always lots of graffiti and we ran into this fifteen-year-old kid named Steve, who was known as ESPO. He was down there starting to do a piece over another guy's work, a Puerto Rican kid from Hunter Park called Karaz LK Lover, who had eccentric habits we assumed were due to some unknown substance, but would definitely fuck some shit up. Karaz's energy was like Fat Joe's, animated and amped. Meanwhile ESPO was this little frail white boy. When we stumbled on ESPO he was just starting to X out the Karaz piece. To cross out someone else's work was exceptionally disrespectful, and wars were launched for less. ESPO was beefing with Karaz, but he didn't want to take the credit or the heat. So ESPO sees us and says, "Yo, y'all want me to throw y'all some cans and get some paint? I'll give you all this shit. All y'all gotta do is X this piece out." We didn't know Karaz personally at that time but ESPO made it sound light—"Oh, he's just some dude I'm beefing with or whatever." So we said "Cool," and bombed all over this guy's piece. We were just hyped to be hanging out with ESPO. Once we'd finished, ESPO took some Polaroids of us in the act, and then some more with us standing in front of the piece. We thought nothing of it.

It's now time for the next meeting, but I couldn't go because I was on punishment. Whenever I got suspended—which was often—I'd have to stay in the crib. Meanwhile the T.E.T. crew goes to the town hall and Karaz comes in, mad as shit. He's ready to fuck ESPO up, like, "Yo, I heard you was X-ing my shit out." But here goes ESPO—"Yo, yo, it wasn't me." And pulls out the pictures. We were little kids to them, and the strength of us being as young as we were and *that* brazen to both bomb a piece *and* pose for photos in the act commanded mad respect from the community. She-Rock and Hammed were the T.E.T. crew members in attendance, and from that moment on they got to get down with the big voices—they were now put on in an official way in the graffiti community. Even though I was partially responsible for having crossed out the piece, after they let those two in the club it was like admissions were over. I missed the meeting and they weren't looking for some other ten-year-old kid to let in the group. And it wasn't like Hammed and She-Rock were like, "Yo, 'Riq did it too." So it was what it was. Those two would go on to get a rep all over the city from writing. And I would be right with them, but I was like Switzerland: just a sovereign individual writer without a real crew.

My days as a graff writer forced me to get really good at shoplifting, because it was frowned upon to pay for your supplies. We would go into art or drug stores, even hardware stores, and grab up spray paint, markers, and tubes of Wite-Out that we could squeeze onto the backs of bus seats—whatever we needed to tag—hide it in our sweatshirts, backpacks, and pockets, and try to walk out unnoticed. We would also take stuff from school and repurpose it. You just couldn't pay to get wherever you needed to go in order to write. So at ten or eleven years old I started hopping the turnstile to get on the train, running through subway tunnels and down train tracks, pulling the wires off the back of the trolley so that when the driver had to get off to reattach the cable, we could sneak on board. Whatever it took.

But I couldn't go too long without consequences. I got picked up by the police for the first time for shoplifting right when I was about to turn twelve. Otis and I got caught taking markers from a supermarket in Center City by an undercover cop. They held us downtown at the station until somebody came to pick us up. It wasn't a jail cell, exactly, but whatever it was felt like a meat locker.

My first actual arrest for graffiti came in the summer of my twelfth year. When we spray-painted graffiti around the way there was always this nosy lady spying on us, watching us from her building across the street from the basketball courts and an abandoned lot that we frequented. She used to sit in the window all the time but was never a threat, because she was old and stayed indoors. But one day her grown son was visiting and he decided to play captain of the block. Peering out the same window, he saw us writing and came running across the basketball courts, yelling. It was me, Hammed, and Hammed's younger brother Faheem, who was about six or seven years old. So we all scattered: Faheem runs one way, Hammed ran another way, and dude picked me to run after. He was like Jesse Owens, fast as a fucking track star, so when he ran up on me I sprayed the paint in his face. So now he was furious and running, eyes burning, and he grabbed me by my shirt but I wiggled away. I finally got to the main street, past the playground and the lot and the courts. A car pulled up into the intersection in front of me, causing me to try to run around it, which slowed me up enough for dude to grab me. And as soon as he got a hold on me, actual police cars pulled up.

The cops put me in the back of the patrol car. By then Hammed had returned with his sister, Kim, who was maybe sixteen or seventeen. Kim is trying to get me out of being locked up, yelling, "That's my son! That's my son y'all got!" But they weren't hearing it. The police were like, "No, you got to come and get him from the fucking precinct." So here I am, twelve, locked up in the precinct in what they called the sweatbox. There was a barred window in there that opened a little bit and the homeys came to see me. My mom didn't even know I was locked up yet, since she was at work somewhere. I was in that hot room for a few hours until she came to get me, and we began to prep for the court date.

It was our family friend Arthur Price who taught me how to appear in court, what to say to the judge, and offered character witness testimony on my behalf. I was ordered to do 150 hours of scrub time, which meant I had to work with an organization called the Anti-Graffiti Network to wash and paint over the graffiti that was popping up like dandelions all over the city. I was relieved; I knew from my half-brother's experiences that people my age could easily be locked up away somewhere. At least I wasn't going to the Youth Study Center or Sleighton Farms, or one of the juvenile facilities I had already seen when we would go to visit Keith. During my scrub time I met Jane Golden, who would go on to become my mentor and evolved the Anti-Graffiti Network into the nonprofit organization Mural Arts, of which I'm currently a board member. Mural Arts is responsible for covering Philly with the public art pieces for which the city is now known and respected. I also was able to meet other graffiti legends, people that I had only known through their tags, who were sentenced to scrub time as well. The hours of work were like riding in a Trojan horse: from the vantage point of the cleanup crews we would know where the freshest, most recently painted walls were—because we were the ones who had made them anew. And we'd share information:

"We painted five walls today, them shits is pretty. It's a joint at this intersection, this intersection."

Then we would come back out at night and hit them up with a band of other renowned artists. That was part of the reason why they started commissioning actual murals, knowing that we were less likely to deface something that was already beautiful. But back then they had us out there using sandblasters and chemicals to clean these walls and paint them burgundy or gray or white. What did they think we were going to do? We're graffiti writers. That shit was calling us and by nightfall we'd be right back to it.

Graffiti art, writing your name on the wall, was actually pioneered in Philadelphia. Even though it was considered one of the pillars of hip-hop alongside rapping and the DJ breaks and the B-boy dance styles, which were all born in the Bronx, graffiti, the visual art aspect, was essentially invented by Cornbread. Known as the King of Walls, Cornbread didn't indulge the stylistic techniques mastered by graff artists who would come after him: hieroglyphic techniques, burner style, wicked style. No—Cornbread just wrote his name in a very rudimentary, almost childlike way, but his name was *everywhere*. It was almost obsessive-compulsive. Using only two colors of paint—silver to show up on a dark wall, and then black to show up on a lighter-colored wall—he became an icon in both the city and the culture, coining the concept of "being all-city," or having your name known all over town from writing. The height of his glory arguably came when Cornbread broke into the Philadelphia Zoo and tagged his name on an elephant. He too went on to work with Jane Golden and do some of the very first murals in the city. Because Cornbread was respected in that way, Jane and her team felt like if he was involved in the beautification of the city then a movement could start. They were right: graffiti, this huge part of Philly culture, gave way to murals. And Mural Arts would become the largest public arts program in the United States.

ART WAS ALWAYS practical escapism for me. My mother's bet from my early age was paying off—visual arts had become a core language of my self-expression, coupled with my new penchant for rapping. I was still introverted, but fearless in the face of this emerging phenomenon called hip-hop. It was giving me the freedom to step into myself by exploring everything I could be: The emcee. The graff artist. The solo act. The crew corraller. The break dancer. The beatboxer. Hip-hop became another more compelling tool in the creative arsenal that Minnie and my mom established, while also allowing me to define for myself who *I* could be, to see myself outside of any boxes I'd known. That was its beauty—it was a medium for taking in and remaking all the possibilities of Blackness. Griots say that the people are never truly aware that they're living in a renaissance, but something in me knew: the changes were visceral, I could feel them in my body. Renaissance and revolution perfumed the air, mixed with the angst of the age. And witnessing the legends warmly open their arms to welcome me and my homies into their fold was only confirmation: we could be whoever we wanted. Whenever we wanted. We just had to show up.

MANUAL LABOR OF THE SCHOLARLY PURSUIT

CHAPTER 12
DOING THE WORK

MY TRIBE WAS PATIENT ENOUGH TO PROTECT ME AS I deepened my capabilities, even when those paths took me outside the law or were penalized by school. They were also wise enough to redirect me when needed. Figuring out a high school in Philly is a unique sport given our blend of charter and public schools, and the violence that can come with the latter. It was Arthur Price who suggested that I go to the Philadelphia High School for the Creative and Performing Arts, known as CAPA. Now located at South Broad, the imposing building looks like a blend of the White House and the Roman Pantheon, its white limestone and jutting columns a small echo of the architecture of the Philadelphia Museum of Art. Back then, it was housed in the Palumbo building in South Philly off Catharine Street, three floors of the most creative folks from Philly in a dusty brick enclosure.

ARTHUR HAD A COUSIN named Bam at CAPA, who I would see on television and at dance recitals. Even as a young person, Bam was the real deal, a Bill T. Jones type, and he was from our hood. I looked up to him, impressed at how serious and driven he was about his art. Bam would eventually become an Alvin Ailey dancer, but back then he was a dance major at CAPA. One of my grandmother's coworkers and fellow churchgoers, a woman named Mrs. Dumpson, had a son named Donald who was one of the vocal teachers at CAPA. If my grandmother was selling dinners to make a little bit of extra money that month, the Dumpson house was one I'd sometimes deliver to, and Donald would always be sitting at their piano, singing. He was the vocal teacher that taught the members of Boyz II Men and encouraged them to become a group. Arthur Price, Donald, and Bam all pushed me to go to CAPA. They knew me as a singer—they were all familiar with my vocal range from my time in church—and suggested that's how I should try to get into CAPA. But I felt more secure in my skill as an artist, because I had been in art schools my whole life and, of course, I'd been honing my skills in the streets, too. I had two auditions at two different schools: the first for Franklin Learning and the second for CAPA. I got into both, but CAPA was my first choice.

As soon as I got there I started having buyer's remorse about my visual arts major. The hallways of CAPA were music central. There were so many genius instrumentalists and singers. There was Christian McBride, Joey DeFrancesco (who after school would play piano for Miles Davis), Amel Larrieux, Fatin Dantzler from Kindred the Family Soul, and fucking Boyz II Men. Everybody there was just . . . *brilliant.* I was surrounded by people who were the best doing what they did at fifteen or sixteen years old. It was alien. Part of me was like, *Damn, I'm glad I didn't try to come here as a singer because I probably wouldn't have made it.* But there was another side that thought, *I should really look into changing my major. Immediately.*

In the end, I decided to just do both. I would do my best

in my art classes, but whenever I had a free moment or an open period I would sit in on music classes.

Mr. Corey was my painting instructor. He was an emo, empathetic, Rick Owens–style character—lean, pale, wore all black. He gave off a vampiric, Lost Boys vibe and we could all tell he smoked weed. But he was an amazing artist and instructor, and his approach resonated with me: there was no line between what Mr. Corey created and who he was as a human. Viewing the canvas as a portal—an invitation to unearth what had long been buried—Mr. Corey laid himself, his emotions, his beliefs, his life, there in his work and pushed us to do the same. Art had been an escape, a fun act of surface-level expression, but with Mr. Corey it became imperative that the art alchemized from the banal materials of paper, canvas, oils, and charcoal a creation that expressed all that I felt. It's an approach that resonates with me now more than ever. Then there was Miss Davis; if that school was *Fame,* Miss Davis was Debbie Allen. She was a bomb-ass dance instructor with a kind spirit that could change the energy of any room she entered. Mr. Cohen, my graphic design instructor, was another teacher who stuck out; I never left his class without learning something that I had never before considered.

Through my ninth- and tenth-grade years my focus was on getting as much out of the school as possible. I would finish my regular coursework early so I could sit in on an instrumental class, or I'd skip gym or lunch to go to a music class. There was a deep curiosity in me, sparked by my desire to exist as more than one type of person—a concept heralded by hip-hop culture. It made me want to know more. Made me want to push myself more. But I was also trying to balance that academic urge with my growing life outside of school walls. My grandmother really stressed the idea of hard work: if you didn't have a job, you needed to be looking for one. I'm from the school of want ads on the back of the newspaper and beating the street. Wake up, leave, look for a job, come home in the evening. With dinnertime came the refrain of:

"Did you find a job?"

"No."

"Alright. Well, you going to go look tomorrow?"

AND YOU KEEP LOOKING till you find one. And I would always find a job. I started working in a restaurant at around thirteen, starting as a dishwasher and eventually ending up around the chefs and sous chefs making the food. The job was fluid. A manager would come in one day and say, "Yo, you're on salads." Or I would be on food prep, so I'd be the one that had to wash all the spinach, put it into these massive buckets with lids, and take it into the walk-in refrigerator. And then come back and chop mad tomatoes or take the shells off of a thousand shrimp. I was doing the tasks like potato peeling, stuff that no one else wanted to do but that allowed the kitchen to work, so that when the chef needs what he needs, he can just go, *boom, boom, boom* and grab it all. Between that and being hungry after school, knowing there's ingredients sitting in the refrigerator, or going to Shawn's crib after school to make our own cheesesteaks and burgers, I learned how to cook.

I also learned how to double my money. When I was younger, I was always thinking, *Yo, I can't wait until I'm fourteen so I can work legally and actually get a check*. And then I turned fourteen and was like, *Damn. I wish I could have stayed undocumented. The government's taking all my money!* So I started running with this dude who would make me my tax money back. When I was in the tenth grade, I worked at the hospital for the elderly called Logan Square East near the Art Museum area. On paydays I would cash my check downstairs at the bank and then I would give my little $300 or whatever to one of the maintenance dudes who worked there. When we got off work he would go downtown and run three-card monte scams and red-foam-ball-under-the-cup scams: pick the red card, the cards move around—*bop, bop, bop, bop, bop*—pick it up, and: "Nope. You lost your money," as slick and fast at "throwin' cards" as the character Lincoln from the play *Topdog/Underdog*. We'd go to the bus station. We'd go to 11th and Chestnut and play the Chestnut Street Market to get the tourists and shoppers coming in and out of the stores. We would hit the arcade at the old bus station on Filbert Street. My job was just to be a plant, the guy who appeared to be winning. It looks like I keep finding the shit and he's giving me money. But the money I'm "winning" is our money that we pool together. By the time we're done and going home, I'd have gone from $320 to $600.

But these jobs were impacting my attendance in school. By the end of my tenth-grade year, I'd missed so many of one of my art classes that the teacher decided to give me a D. I had a high B to an A average in his class on all my assignments and I was a brilliant artist, but he wanted to make an example of me because of my absences. When he gave me the D, I was kicked out of school. Meanwhile the only reason I was missing classes was because I had a job and worked at night, getting off at 3:00 A.M. on the other side of town and having to get *back* down to South Philly and be up and at school by 7:45. It felt like one of those key crossroads in life where had I played the game differently, had I not sold my tokens to make extra money and instead took the bus to school every day instead of walking, I wouldn't have been getting there five minutes late as often as I had. But I didn't think they'd ever do something like that: I was talented, I was an A student. And I thought to myself, *I could fail English, History, Science, Algebra, all that and* still *stay in this school; all they care about is the arts. And I'm an excellent artist, so I'm good.* And that wasn't enough. They were like, "Oh, you got a D in your major. Yeah . . . you know what that means, right?"

That experience is one of the things that makes me a stickler for time now. It's why I show up early, why I'd rather sit in a car for an hour than be late, why I demand that the people I'm around treat time similarly: because I watched this incredible opportunity taken away from me in a split second, based purely on someone else's strict judgment and lack of grace. I was finally in a place where I was fully valued and appreciated, that was expanding my mind and providing the bridge between who I was and who I wanted to be. It was the perfect escape from the streets and a now-deteriorating home life. And just as it came into my hands, it got snatched away. I'm thrown out of Eden and back into the fallen world.

No one ever asked why I was late. No one ever checked in to see why I was working this job. No one ever told me that I had no chances for correction or that my work wouldn't be weighed in consideration and in my favor. At fifteen, the full weight is on my shoulders. Again.

I think that's why I started to love the sound of clock tower bells. There's something about always knowing the time of day, when time is a gift that just floats through the air on the sound of bells. A reminder that someone's always keeping track. The bells from the city's churches allowed me to move through Philly, from one section to the other, and stay on track, even without a watch.

I always wanted to be the best, to excel in any field I explored, but it's like there was always one small flaw, a choice whose consequences kept me in the shadows. Wanting and ready for the big moment but never quite getting there alongside my peers. Never finishing CAPA. Not being recognized for my graffiti skills. Somehow always ejected from the center of the scene and forced to watch from the sidelines as everyone else was progressing in their lives. A constant state of comparison, that consistent thief of joy.

That fervor and disappointment was a testimony to my truth: all I have ever wanted to do was create. And having learned then the power of experimenting with multiple avenues of expression, I wanted the chance to build all the various pieces of me within a tribe who deemed me essential. Who wouldn't leave me behind.

None of that would truly unfold until I met Ahmir Thompson. And maybe that was all that I needed CAPA for anyway.

APPLES TO ORANGES.
BUT YOU NEED THEM BOTH.

CHAPTER 13
AHMIR THOMPSON

AS THE NOW INFAMOUS STORY OF THE FIRST MEETING OF Ahmir and me goes, I had been caught in the school bathroom with one of the ballerinas and was brought into the administration office for a reprimand. Ahmir was also in the office, but he had come in on his top-student tip: "Hey, I just wanted to say what's up, see how everybody's doing, see if anybody needs any apples or anything." I'm sitting there waiting for my scolding and I notice his jacket.

"Yo, who did your jacket?"

Another one of my hustles at the time was selling the style of jacket he was wearing, a hand-painted denim jacket. I was vexed.

"I know ain't nobody else in here doing jean jackets. That's my thing. And where the fuck you get that necklace at?"

Because the necklace he was wearing, this beaded necklace with a fist on it, was another piece I was making and selling.

Ahmir just took the question at face value.

"I got this from my mom. My mom and dad were in a band in the '60s, '70s, and this is something that they were wearing back then. It's authentic. The band was called Congress Alley." And then he went into the whole history of Congress Alley—by the time he was done he'd made them sound like Sly and the Family Stone. I found him strangely fascinating.

Ahmir used to walk around school with this little keyboard sampler making beats. I was curious about it.

"Wow, let me get this straight. You're able to record a song, speed it up, and then loop it. And that's how these dudes make these rap tracks?"

Ahmir started putting me on to where all the samples came from, these deep-cut funk and R&B records I'd never heard of. He had an encyclopedic knowledge of all this obscure music because it was the only kind of music his family let him listen to, along with jazz. They were strict about their musical diet and his. Hip-hop wasn't really allowed into the home. Which was my opening. It was my turn to put him on.

"Yo, you ever hear N.W.A, nigga, Ultramagnetic MCs?"

"No, what's that?"

"Yo, check this out."

His face would screw up while the tape played.

"Oh my God. They're really saying that? Like *fuck*."

"You can hold that tape and take it home."

"No, I can never take this tape home. I'll listen to it here at school in the daytime. If my parents find me with this tape, it's a wrap."

I was shocked. I came from a house where not only was I mostly able to do what I wanted, but I was also able to hide things in the event that what I had would upset an adult.

"Wow, okay, cool, fuck it. Damn, your parents monitor the music you listen to like that?"

His face turned solemn. "You have no idea."

Once I got to know him better, I realized he wasn't lying.

At school he'd spend five hours rehearsing and playing drums, and then he'd go home and have to practice in the basement with the drum kit for another two, three hours. I would get home from school and after a couple of hours I'd call his house. One of his parents always answered.

"Hey, can I speak to Ahmir?"

"Ahmir is practicing." *Click*.

I WAS LIKE, *Yo, they really got you in the basement like that?* Then I go to his house for the first time and notice that they've got bars on the gaddamn windows and a padlock on the inside of the front door. You needed the key to the padlock to get *out* of the house. If you can't find the key and there's a fire, it's a wrap. When I visited, I'd go a little crazy in there just thinking about the fire hazard, based on my own childhood, of course, but also just feeling weird because we were locked inside. They lived in a rough part of West Philly, so some of that protection was to keep what was outside, outside. But it was also to keep Ahmir inside, immersed in his musical studies. He lived and breathed music damn near every waking moment.

We offered a necessary level of escapism to each other. I was deep in the world of hip-hop and rap. Crack was hitting right on my front step and then deep in my mother's veins. I was a part of all of it. There was no keeping the outside, outside. It was in my family, it was in my blood, in my DNA and totally inescapable even as Minnie and our tribe did their best to shield me. And for Ahmir, a kid locked in a basement with a drum kit and jazz on vinyl, I think that was exciting. But I looked at his situation, as extreme as it was, with some envy. He was coming from what appeared to be a stable household. A sister and two parents. Both his parents lived in the crib and they were even in a band together, performing shows on the weekend. I felt like, *Wait, your mom* and *dad live here? Y'all got a car? Yo, Ahmir—you got it made.*

And he'd turn around and say, "So, let me get this straight. You know the gangsters on your block?"

"Yeah, and there's gangsters on your block too."

"I don't know them. I never interact with them."

He walked down Osage Avenue with blinders on. We were polar opposites, meeting at the crossroads of that school. We fascinated each other.

IN MY YOUNG LIFE AS AN EMCEE, I always gravitated towards whoever had the equipment to make music for my rhyming: a DJ or a drummer, anybody with a drum kit, a drum machine, or two turntables. The depth of Ahmir's talent was a double gift for me. He was a musician and could play anything on the drums, but he could also play all of my favorite break beats on the keyboard with the sampler. We were together all the time. I would be in his music classes in CAPA, or sit in at these extracurricular music classes in the jazz program at the Community College of Philadelphia or Settlement Music School, an independent music school in West Philly in a white building tucked behind all the main roads. Wherever Ahmir was being given lessons, I would join him and soak it up. Life in the youth and church choirs made me appreciate the dynamics of a group. I don't know whose idea it was first, but the truth is it felt like Ahmir and I evolved into a group by mutual, silent agreement. It just made sense.

Our group debut was a talent show called Sentimental Journey, an annual event at CAPA that has since been defunded. I had finally settled on my rap name: "Black" came from my skill as a painter. I was fascinated by how the color black was created by blending all the other colors together on your palette, folding the yellows and greens, red and blue pigments into each other to get a shade of pure blackness. It felt like the right metaphor for my life, personally and creatively. "Thought" would follow it, as my intention was to speak my consciousness out loud. It was only over time that I connected those words to ideas of Black pride and critical thinking, but I think that's why the name was perfect. It grew with me.

Ahmir and I had gone to the studio a couple times before we did that first show, pooling our money together for a few recording sessions that cost around fifty dollars an hour and would last maybe three hours at a time. We would get as much done as we could in that time, and ended up creating a couple of demos with the idea of shopping them to labels and executives directly or a few degrees of separation away, on some "if we could just get our tape in the right hands." We had ambition and we were always very detailed in our visioning: what we would call ourselves, who we would sign with, what the album would sound like, what it would look like. We created various mockups of the album—different group names, different album titles, different song lists. And Ahmir was always big on the liner notes. Even before the songs were recorded, or even written, he would create these elaborate liner notes telling stories about a song, hyping up a song that didn't yet exist with a whole narrative of how it came to be. Our vision was clear. We knew what we wanted. We went for it.

But I never trusted the world would make things easy for me.

—

IN THOSE EARLY STUDIO SESSIONS, Ahmir and I first recorded a demo with a song called "PIR: Partners in Rhyme." It wasn't the first time I recorded my voice, but it was the first time I'd done it in a proper studio. Considering that $50-per-hour rate, we didn't have very long to work, but we got this one song done. We each left the studio with a copy of the final mix on cassette. At that point in my life that one song and one cassette, for all intents and purposes, might as well have been my album. It was the first song of the demo we planned to make, a shot to build a creative life away from the chaos of the streets around me. The partnership between Ahmir and me was still very new, and this was the first thing we had done. There was a lot of hope wrapped up in this one track.

I had a big old-school boom box that I bought for seventy-five dollars or so. I'd sit out on the front porch of our house with the boom box next to me, or I'd put it in the open doorway or a window so I could hear the music while I sat outside. I never left it alone, out in the open. On warm spring weekend days, sitting on our porch, I would play that one track over and over again. It was market research: I'd watch to see how niggas on the block were rocking to it. One day I had to leave and do something real quick—maybe run to my aunt's house for an errand—but I kept the music playing so people in the street could maintain the vibe. But when I got back to the block I noticed that the music playing had changed; now I heard a radio station playing whatever the rap show was back then instead of my demo. And the sound quality wasn't the same. The music was coming from somewhere else. As I reached my stoop I could see that my boom box was gone. And the cassette vanished with it. I knew immediately that it was one of my boys—it had to be somebody that I thought was a friend. The word had spread to neighbors and corner boys that I had a tape that I was rapping on, which pulled the haters out or pulled the hate out of my friends. I learned later that it wasn't one of my friends at all, but a guy named Grimace. I knew Grimace was hood, but I thought he was a good guy, or at least he was good with me.

Grimace got his name because he was so black he was purple. He was little bit younger than me, in the seventh or eighth grade, but he was gully, a don't-give-a-fuck-about-anyone, from-the-gutter type bol. I think he stole my box just because he couldn't stand the fact that I had it. The tape was just a bonus. After fighting him to get my box and tape back, the boom box was never the same, like a stolen car found with parts missing or the transmission messed up from someone recklessly misusing it.

The crazy thing about Grimace is that when I was in college, I got word that my half-brother had gotten shot multiple times; somebody had lit him up with an Uzi. Allegedly, it was Grimace. It had nothing to do with our beef growing up but was further confirmation of the man's character: he had envy in his heart. The alleged story was that he shot Keith because Keith teased Grimace in front of some girls he was talking to, the way any oldhead would: "What you doing? You ain't got no game! You talking to them girls, you don't know how to talk to no girls, Grimace. Get out of here." In Keith's mind it was just playful banter—he hit Grimace up with some light disses and then sauntered down the street, already over it. Maybe one of the girls laughed. Grimace was embarrassed enough that he pulled out an Uzi and shot my half-brother. *Laugh now.* Luckily, Keith wasn't killed—doctors took out whatever bullets they could, and he survived.

Despite its reputation as being a dog-eat-dog city, the core of Philly is the innate desire of its people to support one another. I believed that and still do. But Grimace was evidence of another side of Philly that we all struggle with—one where the city tries to prove you wrong. When the ones you thought would support you single-handedly work to erase your success. It's the dichotomy of the hood, and it becomes even more clear when you add a little fame into the mix. That's why a lot of us who leave end up asking: Can you move back to your block? Can you, as a Black entertainer, comedian, artist, ever come home and move through the streets and *not* inspire jealousy? Fear? When does that collective sense of victory turn into private envy? When do people start to blame you for the lives that they live? I wasn't even famous yet when Grimace stole my boom box, but just having a box and a tape with my voice on it was enough to turn his heart against me. That taught me something about the world. My grandmother's omen—"Those boys aren't your friends"—came back to me, now ringing with new truth.

But one stolen box didn't stop the show. Ahmir and I knew exactly what we wanted and were inspired by what felt like a million success stories of people from Philly who had made it big, just through determination and laser focus. There's something in the water in Philly that creates these rags-to-riches narratives—a reservoir of resilience, perseverance, focus, courage, sacrifice, and determination that we all drink from. Or maybe it's just that motherfuckers are desperate to find a way to get out of their circumstances. Philly is a city that seems to exist in this liminal state, a place that makes you who you are and makes you want to be more. But we are fighters.

Coming from my blocks in South Philly with all that I had seen, I wanted out. I watched people kill and die in the street or get entrapped in a system designed to break their spirits. And I knew I would end up one of them too, if I didn't break the cycle. My mother taught me there was more to the city than our stretch of blocks, but within that lesson was a larger one: *The world is bigger than what you know.* The hood would always be there, but opportunities, when they came along, needed to be held on to tightly with both hands.

Imagine if Meek Mill would've just quit because it didn't work out with him and T.I.? His career would've been over and he'd have never made any money. Meek used to hang out in front of the barbershop where I went, asking me if I had any weed: "Yo, oldhead, you got anything to smoke?"

"We ain't got nothing."

"Nah, you be having that crazy shit."

His first deal was as an artist under Charlie Mack's production company, which didn't work out. And then he signed with T.I., and that didn't work out. But he didn't stop trying after either of those initial deals that went sour, and when he found the right connection—with Rick Ross—his life changed forever.

Kevin Hart—he wasn't a good comedian when he first started. It's true. Niggas in Philly did not think he was funny. Imagine if he listened to the haters and stopped coming up to New York, stopped getting onstage at clubs. Nah, he kept it moving. You have to commit and ride it out. You don't always determine the schedule and the timing of your breakthrough. All that's in your control is your commitment to your dream.

THAT'S WHAT EVERY ONE of those ups and downs taught me. Every missed chance, every opportunity snatched away, made me hungrier for the next one, more focused and clear about who I was and wanted to be, and more *patient*. It took me a minute to grasp it, but there's so much power in a state of patience. I honed my craft in that time of waiting and worked on myself in a deeper way. I grew to understand how to respond to setbacks with grace and acceptance, even when the doubt started to kick in. Because there have definitely been times when I've doubted, at every point in my career. When we were on a festival bill and felt like another performer was outshining us. The times we felt stalled and considered doing some bullshit to get popular and get money. If left unchecked, doubt can turn into paralyzing fear. But you have to keep the vision in mind: as Katt Williams says, "Make your decisions from your talent, not your desperation." (I can't believe I'm quoting Katt Williams.)

But from the start, Ahmir wasn't afraid, and neither was I. Through his parents, he could see the possibilities of what it meant to live a creative life. He was training for it, day and night. In many ways that dedication rubbed off on me and made me want to push with everything I had. He would show up in the moments where I faltered and could have fallen off. And we were aligned in the art of it all. In the earliest stages of the band I was always over his house, watching the same two movies: *Do the Right Thing* and *Cape Fear.* Between '89 and '91, Ahmir and I watched those movies probably a fucking thousand times. We were beyond best friends. We had become brothers, and Ahmir's mom became another mother figure to me. I came over at any time and stayed as long as I wanted. I could stay for thirty nights in a row and when his parents would say to me, "Maybe you need to go home," Ahmir would come and stay at my crib. We were together every day, all day, in person or talking on the phone, trying to figure out how it's going to be when we get on. *Here, listen to this record. Here, listen to this rhyme. Let me put you on with this.*

We stayed like this for years. The only thing that would ever come between us was a fight. It was in London. Ahmir writes about it in his book, *Mo' Meta Blues: The World According to Questlove*. This was when I was still running hot, still following the code I had adapted to in South Philly: the idea that when you disagree, you fight it out, even viciously, even among friends, and then you let it go. Ahmir had been sheltered from that level of chaos, and rightfully so. The fight was over something relatively small: he hadn't included my name in the credits of a track, after I had spent time in the studio helping to produce it and had specifically asked to make sure that it was credited back to me. When we got to the London offices of our label and looked at the LP, my name wasn't there. Malik B., another member of the group, sort of hyped it up, like "Ooooh, can't believe they did that shit, what you gonna do, 'Riq?!"

I confronted Ahmir about it in my loud, pissed-off, in-your-face South Philly way. We were in a glass office in London with all these people looking on as Ahmir and I got into a brawl, tussling and rolling around on the floor, punches being thrown. Ahmir was larger than me, so it ended up being more a wrestling match than a square-off, and it ended with me walking off, pissed. Ahmir, on the other hand, was shocked—it was probably the first fight he had ever had in his life. I was twenty years old, we were brothers, and for me it was a totally normal way of getting my frustration out and point across. But it unsettled Ahmir to his core.

Ten minutes later I was back on the phone trying to find somebody to send us some Philly blunts from the States, because we couldn't find our cigars over there. I didn't even really care about the record, about the credit, none of that, anymore. It was all out of my system. As soon as we got back to the flat, Malik started telling the rest of our crew what happened: "Yo, y'all missed it. We was fighting up in the label. You know what I'm saying? 'Riq hit Ahmir. He busted his lip." And a refrain from the crew: "Oh shit. What? He busted him in the lip?!" The others on the trip—Kamal and Rich and Joe and everybody else—came from the same mindset as me: you can fight today and then go back to being boys again tomorrow. Now they were all chiming in about the fight, blowing it up, which I think embarrassed Ahmir and made him feel the whole event in a deeper way.

To hear him tell it, he never held a grudge. But it would always color our relationship. I watched him retreat deeper into himself, and my grandmother's words rang true again. Even close friendships could change, and this one changed in ways I never expected. Over the following years, we both cliqued up with different people, but he wasn't just looking for new creative partners—he searched for that same brotherly dynamic and energy we had, but now with others, people I wasn't working with. That was the impetus for his forming the Soulquarians, bonding with D'Angelo and with Mos Def and Talib Kweli and Common and other rappers. Sometimes I would feel like, *Why them? You already got the best rapper right here.* My loyalty to Ahmir never changed. That is my brother. But in that moment of physical conflict between us, a boundary had been both violated and reaffirmed: he and I were different. I was too young to understand the long-term implications of my reaction, but I started to realize that in this new life, I needed to unlearn South Philly's training.

But even with our differences, our shared vision never wavered and still hasn't. I was only in school for ninth and tenth grade, and by my sophomore year Ahmir was a graduating senior. It was after he left for his senior project that I got kicked out. But that was all the time that we needed together in that school, because the seed had been sown. We knew who we were. We were a group.

THE HOUSE THAT HAUNTS ME

CHAPTER 14
AN EPIDEMIC

AS I WAS GAINING CLARITY ON MY LIFE'S POTENTIAL, Philly was twisting deeper into a nightmarish reality with the onset of crack. On South Philly's narrow streets children would play on the pavement with dusty colored chalk, marking geometric fields for games like hopscotch and skully. I loved playing skully: Someone would draw a box onto the pavement and we'd make little pucks from found bottlecaps filled with smoothed and flattened street tar or resin—we'd slide our pieces across the box, trying to knock our opponents' pieces out of bounds. You'd walk to the edge of the box, your field drawn before you and the competitive rush sinking in, and when you achieved your aim you'd yell, "Skully!" On another block there might be girls playing double Dutch, the *tit-tat* swirl of the ropes inspiring them to create new stepping rhythms. One year, when I was ten or so, I spent damn near the whole summer sitting on the front steps and playing checkers against my neighbor from across the street on his oversized wooden board, with different neighbors joining in from time to time.

On those little streets, you'd see the full spectrum of young Black joy on vivid display. We weren't allowed to stay in the house. You had to go outside and be engaged; there was no way to avoid it (which, in retrospect, was a good exercise that gave me the few social skills I do have). Our parents weren't worried. We would watch them come and go in steady streams to and from work, interior lights flicking on up and down the block around the same time as they entered and prepared for the evening. In that era of South Philadelphia there was always some level of violence, but never a lot of brutality. Somebody might get stabbed or have their face cut with a razor, but people mostly fought with bottles and chains on their *West Side Story* vibe, rather than with guns or machetes or burning people's houses down—all that came later, with the drug wars and the despair and the ruthlessness of addiction.

When crack flooded Philly, our street changed. Kids couldn't be outside and play as often, and when we did go out, we were definitely not carefree. We were out there hungry, or cold, or deserted. Crack fractured my entire generation as we watched this new drug demolish the structure of our lives down to its foundations. So many of us began to have to do for self and figure it out, years before any normal child should have to. We were parenting our parents or losing them altogether. No one had ever seen an addict like the crack fiend—their willingness to do *whatever* in order to get the next hit overwhelmed everything else in their lives. The powerful motivation of unconditional love and concern for their own children wasn't enough to break through the vise-like grip of the high.

Crack didn't differentiate between sexes, races, or creeds. Anybody could get it, and likely everybody *would* get it at some point, it cut through our hood with such a wide swath. There was a lot of variation and range in the demographics of people who you would find out had smoked crack. It's like today, how we all watch something go viral but don't understand why everybody's doing it. Why did eighty-five million suddenly start planking or dumping ice buckets over their head, or doing some silly dance or lip sync? That was crack. The epidemic was the algorithm, and after a certain point it seemed to have a mind of its own. Forget those *Goodfella*-style mafia movies where the Italians nobly declare that they would only sell drugs to Black communities: there were strips everywhere, all over the city. A crazy time to be alive.

There were multiple ripple effects. Kids who were thirteen or fourteen who were slinging would go from poverty to thousandaires or even hundred-thousandaires, driving BMWs before they were old enough to have a license. You might see a kid, barely out of middle school, driving a Mercedes, all kitted up and customized, wearing a big fucking huge rope chain and Gucci links. Everybody my age was trying to eat. I even tried selling. It didn't matter to me because I already had a job and my heart wasn't in it, but I still tried because that was what you did at the time. Forget the money, for a second, sometimes drug dealing was just for optics. Making money from a square job wasn't enough—back then, chicks wanted that little bit of danger to be down. If I wanted chicks, it behooved me to look like one of those boys in the hood. I wasn't anything close to a kingpin or one of the true getting-money niggas, but I kept fresh sneakers, had my little gold teeth. I kept working at the old folks' home and progressively getting just enough money not to become dependent on dealing. Which was good, because I was terrible at it.

A customer would come up and ask me, "Yo, you got anything?" and I'm like, "Yeah, here." I'd have five caps in my hand and let them pick out the one they wanted—but the smart fiends with quick hands know they can take a good one, plant a bad one in my hand, and then be like *Oh nah, I'm good,* leave with the good cap and leave me with the spent one. The whole transaction would be a failure. But I didn't care at all. It got to the point where even my mom told me, "Yo, word on the street is that you sweet, nigga." In other words, *What is you doing out here?*

BY NOW MY MOM was on the shit too. I saw my mother, someone who had always been a provider and an earner and a hustler, someone always able to go out and get it, start to falter in ways she never had before. In our house we were surviving off of free government cheese—we were lucky that my grandmother worked in the office that gave out government assistance, so she made sure we were on the list. But Minnie was an honest woman, so we only got what was coming to us and not a bit more. There would be days where we'd run out and I'd have to go to a friend's or an aunt's house with a note asking them for a little bit of theirs. On a lucky week we got one extra block.

It wasn't just my mom. While the corner boys who could actually deal drugs got their come-up and the rest of us dabbled for show, everybody else in the neighborhood turned into zombies—or "pipers," as we sometimes called them (you smoke a pipe, you're a piper). There wasn't a family untouched: someone in your lineage was smoking crack. It might be someone everyone knew, the man who was always neat and responsible and had a good job, but then one night at a party someone convinces him that crack is basically the same as powder cocaine and he hits that shit. And that was it. There was no coming back. For teenage boys, if there was a grown woman in the neighborhood a boy was attracted to and wanted to get at, all he had to do was wait until she got on the pipe and then everybody had their shot. For a lot of boys their first sexual experiences during that time—from losing their virginity to getting oral or maybe "running the train" on someone—were with addicts: women who were addicted to the drug and needed a little bit of money to go and get another hit and would do anything for it. The woman could be anyone, maybe your best friend's mom or your mom's girlfriend who you always called your auntie, but now young boys were with those women doing what they called *trickin'*. Addicts left kids at home alone while they were out trying to find their next fix. It gave rise to the grandparent family dynamic, as grands stepped in to raise their children's babies, to make sure that they too wouldn't be lost to the streets. Crack decimated structures that were only just stabilizing after the civil rights era.

Underneath all of this was a deeper layer of violence. Teenage boys were killing each other, but old people, young people, the disabled—anyone in a more vulnerable position—were also more susceptible to being preyed upon. You would see it play out in real time and in broad daylight, with no one stepping in to help. Or even worse, you would hear the sounds of violence and pleading or pain in the darkness of night and only find out what actually happened the next morning or afternoon. If things really got out of hand, you'd see it on the news or read about it in the paper.

Sundays brought the smokers to church, at least the ones who were struggling to kick it and trying to save themselves and their families. It might also be an addict's only refuge and safe haven for a hot plate of food. But even the sanctuaries could become just another place for a hustle as the pipers worked to find a come-up or do something that might warrant a small tip, like helping carry bags or groceries. Meanwhile more and more children were coming to church by themselves.

There was so much that we normalized in those days, the perfect recipe for trauma and PTSD.

IT FUCKED ME UP to see my mom like that, lost in this world of chaos. But I had resigned myself to the fact that my mother was a grown woman. I would have to stop trying to parent her. Two things brought me there: the first is that she would disappear for days at a time. On one occasion, when I was around fourteen, I heard that she was in this crib, a drug house, a few blocks away. I go to the spot, knock on the door, and motherfuckers are in there getting high as hell.

I asked the person who answered the door, "Yo, is Cassie in there?"

"I don't know."

So I walk in and I'm searching the house, going into these different rooms trying to find her. It's not the Four Seasons. It's a crack house. In shambles. I find her in one of the rooms and try to grip my mom up.

"Come on. I'm taking you home."

I'm trying to pull her out of the house with all my might. She's kicking, screaming, feet up in the air, not wanting to leave at all. I keep pulling until all the strength just flows out of me. Defeated. So I left her in there. I left her in the fucking crack house. I went back home, got a little pistol I had, and came back and shot out the front window. That was a moment of true clarity. The realization wasn't that she was on her own, but that I was.

Nobody got hurt when I fired into that house, but someone very well could have. I didn't care in that moment. Not at all. I had lost her, fully. I loved her and wanted her back, but the woman who would fight for me was gone. Returning home, I tried not to think about it for a long time. It was hard to even wrap my mind around it, because this was the woman that I never questioned, never doubted. Who I knew I could count on. And she had deliberately chosen not to be that person, not anymore.

The second thing that happened was that my mom popped up again at Minnie's house after we hadn't seen her for a couple days, wearing this T-shirt that was tied up so she was showing midriff and you could see her little belly. I was annoyed—like, *What the fuck? What are you doing? You're out here in jean shorts and shit, your shirt all tied up.* I said, "You're out here looking like a freak joint"—or "a hottie" or something; I don't remember my exact wording, but I definitely didn't say *You a hoe,* I softened it a little bit—but whatever I said, it wasn't the move. It set both her and my grandmother off, even though my grandmother wasn't very happy with her either, at the time. But now they joined forces and pushed me down into my late grandfather's recliner. They held me down and proceeded to fuck me up. There was a lazy Susan that would have nuts and candy on it on the dining room table, and they took the sharp-ass metal lid off that and started whacking my legs. My mom would hold me and my grandmother would get at me with the lid, and then they would switch, both of them rolling on me for acting like I was grown and trying to tell my mom what to do. After that I was like, *You know what? You got it. Just do you. You want to get high? Get high.*

IT'S HARD TO EXPLAIN to anyone how heavy those memories are. It's hard to recall them. I both repress those memories and gloss over them. The fine details are too disturbing. My PTSD from that time manifests itself more in my everyday home life: I don't like slamming doors or drawers because of all the gunshots I heard back then. There was so much gunplay on the block and in the neighborhood. Unnecessary cries and unwarranted screams remind me of the horrors we heard being committed in broad daylight or when we were trying to sleep. The sounds of exhaust fans and fans in general trigger me too, for reasons I don't fully understand. There's a train that passes my house a couple times a day, extremely fast and loud. It can startle me off my seat, even though I know, every day, that it's coming.

A FRESH START,
A BRIEF GLIMPSE OF
A SUNRISE

CHAPTER 15
NEW CITY, NEW SELF

BY THE TIME I WAS FIFTEEN OR SIXTEEN YEARS OLD, MIN-nie could see that it was only a matter of time until I got caught up in something that would fully derail my life. I had been arrested twice between eighth and ninth grade, my half-hearted attempts at selling crack were ongoing, and my mother was lost to the streets, which would give any child a little less to lose. South Philadelphia had shifted, seismically. What, pre-epidemic, had felt like a community now felt like a war zone, and Minnie sensed that it was time for me to be around strong masculine figures for more direct guidance.

First, she sent me to live with Howie, her ex and my biological grandfather, who they thought could help me get my act together. He and his wife, Laverne—we all called her Verne—lived way up in West Oak Lane. The commute from their house to my high school in South Philly was an hour at least, every morning. Verne didn't really like me because I was the grandchild of the first wife, which created a palpable tension in the house. Despite my bond with Howie, it wasn't maybe two months before he had to ask me to leave on account of Verne, which felt incredibly disrespectful considering that I had upended my life on what felt like his suggestion and agreement. We had been talking about colleges and how he was going to give me one of his janky cars to help, but Verne deaded all of that. Howie came to me and revealed that Verne wanted me gone: "Verne is tripping, but my hands are tied."

Somehow, after the West Oak Lane move failed, the collective familial wisdom was that my father's oldest brother, Uncle Cliff, would be able to offer more stability. I had already spent a lot of time around my Uncle Luqmaan, but he was busy doing his thing. I was beyond Luqmaan too, which he realized. He hoped that maybe if I met my other uncle, my father's other brother, a man I'd never met in my life, he might talk some sense into me.

BUT CLIFF WAS IN DETROIT. I had never even been on an airplane. Learning that I was moving to Detroit was random and shocking—but it was also kind of intriguing. It was like, *Wow, this . . . might be fun and fly. He's got a swimming pool? Driving a BMW? Hold on—what is he doing out there?* I felt like the Fresh Prince of Bel-Air. My mom knew I was leaving, but she was smoking crack so she didn't care much: "Yeah . . . yeah, I think that's the best move. Just go and get out of South Philly." She was on the streets but maybe, in hindsight, she was actually a little tuned in. She knew intimately how dangerous Philly had become, and she and Minnie had always been aligned on the direction my life needed to take; both had always been committed to me gaining exposure that eclipsed the one-hundredth-of-a-block perspective that our hood offered.

And then there was Ahmir. We had saved a few hundred dollars and booked a studio session that we'd been looking forward to for some time. But the session was scheduled on the same day that my Uncle Earnest and my grandmother decided that I was moving to Detroit, springing this on me with no warning. Ahmir was waiting for me at the studio, but I'm not there. He calls Minnie's house and she answers.

"He moved, baby. Tariq lives in Detroit now."

Ahmir's like, "What the fuck?" Now, if I was Ahmir, I probably would've been like, *Fuck it, I quit. I'm a classically trained musician, I have no time for this.* But he didn't give up on the dream. We talked a few days later and he asked me, "This thing of ours that we're working on—do you want to keep doing it? I'm down to keep going, near or far." I was deeply moved. My respect for him as a human, beyond my respect for his dedication to the craft or how I admired him as a musician, grew with that one conversation, that one decision to stay locked in. There had not been a clearer moment that showed that we were destined to do whatever it was that we were going to do. In truth, it was me who left for Detroit thinking, *Well, I guess that's it. I'm going to be from Michigan now and be a rapper here.* No one had made it seem like I was coming back to Philly at all, so as far as I knew this move was permanent. But here was Ahmir, even more committed to the vision that we set out to accomplish, despite the shift.

I GOT TO DETROIT and Cliff couldn't talk any sense into me either. How could he? That dude was balling himself. A criminal running a fraudulent company, my uncle was getting money from people for some vague description of services provided: "risk management," he called it. He was taking money, running scams, doing crazy shit. My guess is that given that back in the day my father was back and forth to Chicago stealing cars and scamming and Uncle Earnest was in Philly running a crew of nondescript, discreet bad guys, they probably sent Uncle Cliff to Detroit to stay out of trouble, or be their Midwestern arm. Based on what Luqmaan said about going to Detroit and seeing how Cliff was living, he probably figured out what he was doing but paid it no mind. But whatever Cliff was up to would eventually lead him to being run out of Michigan and dipping to the Dominican Republic.

But while I was there, Detroit offered me a glimpse of what freedom could look like. I was able to drive my uncle's car, make full use of the house and pool, and live in my own apartment at the top of their house with its own separate entrance. My uncle's family didn't need me to work or contribute to the house. I didn't know anyone in the city and wasn't trying to. For a moment it felt like real peace. But once again trouble found me, this time in the form of my cousin, Cliff's daughter, who desperately wanted to live in the apartment I now inhabited and was jealous that she couldn't. After weeks of direct digs and tension mounting, she eventually came to the house ready to stab me.

Back to Philly I went.

A LOSS.

CHAPTER 16
ALONE.

UPON MY RETURN, I WENT TO LIVE WITH MY PATERNAL grandparents in Mount Airy, staying above them in the upstairs duplex apartment my mother and I used to live in before we moved to South Philly. My rent-free stay came with fair conditions: that I paid my utilities, that I would get accepted into and go to college, and that once I went away to school, if I wanted to continue to keep the apartment, I would have to start paying rent. Never one to struggle to get a job, I took up telemarketing gigs at a company called The Data Group in the Plymouth Meeting suburbs and started working at the hospital, on top of going back to school. My utilities weren't crazy—only electric, gas, and telephone bills—so the responsibility wasn't difficult.

Although Detroit didn't change my life, being there and in Mount Airy offered me just enough distance from South Philly to gain clarity and perspective. I finally left the crack dealing to the dudes who really wanted that. And I had to make strategic decisions about which high school to now attend for my junior year. After being kicked out of CAPA, I had gone to my local South Philly high school, but returning home and living in the North and Northeast parts of Philly gave me the option to attend Germantown High School. A friend from elementary school attended GHS, so I wasn't totally alone. They weren't into the reckless life of the era and had my back. Being an outsider at Germantown meant that I would get targeted by some of the students, but it also kept me out of the politics there. I knew who I knew, and that was enough. South Philly High, on the other hand, had been wildly dangerous. There were fights, stabbings, and shootings damn near every day from warring factions and gangs, whose battles over drug territory now spilled over into classrooms since the hood generals were teenage boys. The neighborhood's melting pot experiment had gone awry. Guns were the new weapon of choice, and narcotics created clear combat lines between fighters grouped together by race, creed, and/or block. It was too hot. I knew that spending any extended period of time at that high school would probably lead to me getting roped into battles that weren't my own, through old alliances and expectations.

My only return to South Philly would be my monthly pilgrimage to meet my mom. I used to get a Social Security check and a Veterans Affairs check at the beginning of every month from my father's benefits, and I had to meet up with her to cash them, take my monies out, and give her hers. Beyond that, we kept in touch throughout the month, but it wasn't uncommon for her to just disappear for days at a time. I'd hit up my family, letting them know I hadn't heard from her for a couple of days or a week, and they would always have news: "Oh, it's all good, she went out to one of those neighboring counties and got arrested." In Philly we were leery of leaving the hood to go to the outskirts of town or what we call "the county": the Main Line by West Philly and Cheltenham and Jenkintown or Allentown, north of Mount Airy. There were fewer Black folk in the county, and the police were more likely to wonder what you're doing there and run your plates and license for any warrants. All your paperwork had to be straight if you were out driving through those counties. And if they weren't, then you stay your ass in South Philly, North Philly, Germantown, wherever. You don't cross those lines, and you damn sure don't cross them casually. So my mom would be out there in the county up to no good, doing scams or God knows what, and she would get picked up. That's when she would call Uncle Reds or Uncle Willie to come bail her out, and all would be well again. No questions asked. But for some reason, she would always go back.

After one of these disappearances, though, I called the family and no one had heard from her. In our family, when we couldn't get in touch with someone for a few days, we would first check the precincts to see if they were arrested, then the hospitals to see if they were hurt, then the morgues. I had spoken to her a few days before she disappeared and she sounded cool. She had left a message on my answering machine that she wanted to get with me. I think one of my checks had come in. I heard the voicemail and was going to link with her, but I was working doubles trying to make some extra money, so my days weren't free until the weekend. A lot of the nights after I got off work from my telemarketing job in Plymouth Meeting, this white lady who was a manager there and had a little thing for me would let me drive her car, which is how I learned how to properly drive. But when I had finally freed up, I hadn't heard back from my mom.

So my aunts and uncles went through the motions—the police, hospital. Nothing. When they called the morgue they discovered that a Black Jane Doe body had turned up, but it had been beaten beyond clear recognition. My grandmother,

Aunt Blanche, and Uncle Fonzo all went to see the body, but it didn't help—there was no way to confidently identify a body that had been so mutilated, so we had to wait for the dental records to come back to confirm that it was or wasn't my mother. Both my grandmother and Aunt Blanche knew it was her. The rest of us were hopeful that it wasn't.

I had a girlfriend at that time who was seventeen and a student at Bryn Mawr College. She was militant, raised by a mother who was an educator and activist, and had put me on to lots of music: Bob Marley, Nina Simone, Fela. Waiting for those dental records to come back, I numbed out after a certain point. It was surreal. I felt like I was floating, just going through the motions, disembodied from the physicality of this plane. I remember one day, going outside and just lying in the grass. I had a Sony Walkman and I was listening to a bunch of artists that my girlfriend had put me on to, immersing myself deep into the music, smoking a little bit of weed. I needed to somehow escape my reality. I spent time at her room at Bryn Mawr. She was a huge support for me—she let me know that if the news came back that the corpse was my mom, then we were just going to deal with it together.

I had also moved back in with Minnie for the days we waited.

And then the results came back.

That mutilated body? It was my mom.

SO MANY PEOPLE descended on my grandmother's house. It was the only time in my life that I could remember both sides of my family being in the same space at the same time. When my mother and I lived on Sharpnack Street my father's parents would occasionally come from Jersey to visit and hang out for a while. My grandfather would pull out his dentures and scare me or make me laugh with how few teeth he had left in his mouth. Aside from that, there was almost a separation of church and state between my maternal and paternal sides. But the day the news broke about my mother, they all came together to make sure that I didn't lose it, which is what everyone feared would happen. It's what I always thought I would do, too; I'd been known to say that if I ever lost my mom I would go crazy, *I'm fucking shit up, I'm going to be a savage.* And my entire lineage came that day to make sure that I was okay.

I wasn't. But I wasn't going crazy. I was just numb. I had lost so many other people, close friends, relatives, taken away by violent murder. Everybody else in the family was a wreck, emotional and crying. I wasn't any of those things.

I didn't shed a tear until I saw her body being lowered into the ground. My mother's funeral had to be closed-casket because of what had been done to her body in the course of her murder. So, without having to stare at the body, we had all been doing okay until the casket began its descent. In that moment, my grandmother snapped. She tried to jump in the ground after her daughter, throwing herself on the polished wooden coffin. This was Minnie, who had only shed a single tear when her second husband was also lowered, who was a rock in the hardest of hardships, helping so many other people and their families cope, my Minnie. I never saw her break. Teary-eyed, maybe twice, but to watch her become hysterical shook me up. My half-brother, Keith, was brought to the funeral from another stint in prison, handcuffed and accompanied by marshals. He was allowed to pay his respects before returning to jail. Later we talked on the phone. He tried to paint this picture of "We're all we got" and that he would be out soon. But I had already lost Keith, all those years ago on the sidewalk staring up at our burned and smoking house while he was taken away in a cop car.

My hand in hers.

In those moments I had made a vow to protect and keep her from harm, knowing it was only me and her, but that as long as we had each other, we'd be okay.

Now there was only me.

YEARS OF WATCHING her decline had brought me closure before the soil hit her casket. When I was six, there were parts of me, subconscious maybe, that marked my fiery mistake as the beginning of the unraveling of my family. In those parts of my mind I internalized a simple narrative: it was my fault. But by the time I was sixteen I'd seen too much. Watching my mom fight me when I tried to take her to safety, seeing her whole character change and shift in the sickness of addiction, watching the way that one tiny rock could be cataclysmic in a community—I had no room left for the childlike naïveté that made me think I could keep the world away from us. That believed the illusion that I had control. By now I knew: there was no control, and that realization offered me a taste of freedom. I had done all that I could. I had stayed true to my word and my promise to try and protect her as best I could. I had learned the power of surrender and release. I'm still working to perfect it, but my *patience* guides me.

All I can control is me. Time and time again, after moments of struggle I had no choice but to surrender to the tides of life and their natural rhythms. Childhood and adolescence taught me to be comfortable giving all that I could. For my mother, that was love, even if, after a while, I had to offer it from a distance. It was respect, despite what she changed into right in front of my eyes. I had to learn the power of loving someone still, despite, through, and even *because* of all that they became. There's no control in that power, but there is the consolation of radical acceptance and the life-giving force of unconditional love.

AND SO OUR HEALING BEGAN. My girlfriend came to the funeral, and Minnie allowed her to stay with me at her house. All my cousins and uncles were shocked and awed that I was dating this beautiful college woman *and* that Minnie was letting her stay in the house. But I think, being in South Philly, Minnie was probably wise enough to know that it was better to have someone in the house who would keep me out of the streets. And for her own healing, she wanted me close, too. My grandmother went to therapy for a while, provided by an organization called Families of Murdered Victims. I didn't go to all the sessions, but I accompanied her when they had an extended family meeting. And day by day, both Minnie and I worked on healing together.

Arthur Price's presence and wisdom also helped. There was a tranquility about him, a certain grace he was able to bestow upon me in those moments. His presence is still important to me. Minnie passed in 2020, and I talked to Arthur at length about all of the emotions that her passing brought up and the strain it caused on already fraught family relationships. Arthur told me to listen to what was on my heart: "Do what you feel is best for you to do, and it's going to be in the family's best interest, too." I'm sure he shared a similar sage word around my mother's death, one that helped me glean perspective and heal in a more assured way.

The trial would be the true test. They caught the guy who

killed my mother almost immediately. He was twenty-two or twenty-three years old, living in South Philly, but none of us had ever heard of him. The hearing arrived at the end of my senior year of high school—he was held for a while before the case went to court—and I accompanied my grandmother to the courtrooms at City Hall. My half-brother, still incarcerated, was allowed to come to the proceedings, at the beginning, at least. But when he got there he tried to attack the defendant in the courtroom, as happens with many loved ones when confronting the killer, and was taken away. Having to sit through the gory details of my mother's final moments was tough. I wasn't trying to hear any of it, but I had to be there for the rest of my family and especially for Minnie, who was going no matter what. We hoped he would get a life sentence, but there was a clerical error between the time the trial ended and the sentencing, and for some reason he had to be retried. So we had to sit through all of the awful details—the displays of her bloody clothes, crime-scene photos, *she was strangled with the cord from this lamp, this is the knife, this is her blood all over the killer's sneakers, this is her blood on his clothes*—twice. At the end of the second trial he was given a long sentence, a string of football numbers that equated to life behind bars.

My mother's murder could've been a life sentence for me, too, but instead it became a driving force, pushing me further down the path I'd already entered, pushing me to take it as far as I could. I was determined that the cycles of violence, of being in the streets, of losing what I loved to the beast of South Philly would end with my story. But I was delusional: I've since come to realize that they never really leave you.

THE PRESENT IS THE PRESENT.

CHAPTER 17
THE [SQUARE] ROOTS

I BEGAN RECLAIMING MY FUTURE BY FOCUSING ON MY present. I knew exactly what I had to do. Sticking with this music thing and finishing what I had begun became my tribute to her. Here I was, again, turning to art to create a new beginning after a devastating end. Making music allowed me to transmute my pent-up emotional energy into another essence, one that could flow into the environment around me and connect to others. People could vibe out to my voice. Get lost in my words. Our music provided a way out, even if only for the length of a song, from the ugliness of reality. I might not have articulated all of these ideas so clearly then, but even without words, this knowing settled into me as a responsibility.

Ahmir and his parents and sister became like my extended family, helping me deal with the loss but also helping me dedicate myself to deepening my craft. So much had happened in a short burst of time. I had left for Detroit and moved back. I had hopped around to a bunch of different Philly high schools trying to finish up my education. My mother was killed. Ahmir went to college, and later I went to college. But through all of that, we were a band.

Minnie always supported me as a musician and as an artist. But when I first started writing raps she made it known to me that she disagreed with the lyrics. There was something lost in translation when she would find my rap books lying around and page through them. The profanity didn't read well. She'd come to me and ask, "What is these songs? It's vulgar." Now, I heard Minnie curse a lot, but only when she was angry—in her everyday speech she tried to be more godly. But even during those days when she didn't like my lyrics, she was supportive. She was there from day one at all our shows. Anything that she could pull up to, she would pull up. From the times that it was us just casually playing on the street and holding out a hat for money, to the days when we graduated to shooting music videos.

While I finished high school, Ahmir and I started doing shows as The Square Roots, recruiting different instrumentalists to join us as we busked in South Philly. But when I graduated, as promised to my grandparents, I enrolled in Millersville University, about an hour and a half outside of Philly, for a year. It was a racist town, where the cops would target us for the pettiest crimes; jaywalking was their favorite. I was constantly getting accosted and realized, after one more arrest for not walking in the crosswalk, that it was probably time to go. Once again, though, a short stint at school allowed me to meet an important collaborator: Malik B., who was also attending Millersville.

Hip-hop had gotten bigger and bigger with each passing year, and we were hearing about and connecting with artists from New York who were killing it. They often had more than one emcee and a tag-team flow that brought a new energy to the stage. After seeing Supernatural and Rahzel at a nightclub in Queens, I came back to Philly adamant that we needed another rapper. In walks Malik B.

We would both leave Millersville and transfer to Temple, back in Philly, him a semester earlier than me. Ahmir was also in the city, and that's when we really started to grind it out as a group. We were performing everywhere we could, in a move I learned when my crew was getting an "all-city" rep as graffiti writers: no spot was too small and every place could get it. We killed it at an amateur talent night at a sometimes strip club called the Princess Lounge in North Philly. The host of Drexel University's hip-hop radio show, AJ Shine, along with the iconic Philly DJ Cosmic Kev—who launched the careers of so many people from Philly, like Meek Mill, Jahlil Beats, Peedi Crakk, and other rappers and hip-hop producers—were the judges that evening and they were blown away. We had the strip club jumping, me and Malik blending our lyrics and flow with Ahmir's ability to cover any known break beat in existence on the drums. The audience was rocking to the familiarity of their favorite songs, now played live and blended into some other dope shit they didn't know. It was electric.

The following week we had a performance at the Chestnut Cabaret on the University of Pennsylvania's campus. AJ Shine and Cosmic Kev came and brought with them someone else who would change our lives: Rich Nichols. AJ was excited, like, "There's someone I want y'all to meet. Rich is my guy, he works at Temple as a jazz DJ." But as he kept excitedly talking, I focused on Rich. He was dressed in all black and standing in this dark-ass DJ booth and I thought, *Damn . . . this dude is Black as shit! I thought I was Black, and I'm Black Thought, but he's five shades blacker than me and dressed like the Omen.* After AJ finished his spiel, my honest reply was "Okay, where's he at? You literally brought a fucking shadow."

But Rich was real. He was instrumental in helping us

hone our sound, look, and vibe as a group. He was beyond knowledgeable of the world: of people, of art and music, jazz in particular. He appealed to Ahmir and me for different reasons. Ahmir and Rich could connect on obscure cuts of music, on sonic resonance and tone. Their dialogues on the conceptual aspects of music allowed both of them to share and grow. Rich and I connected on other ideas. He and his wife elaborated on the education and information that my college girlfriend had given me, sharing books about nutrition, metaphysical spirituality and Kemetic consciousness, the origins of Pan-Africanism. He was an all-around creative in his own right, too: a court-deposition cameraman by day and the radio host of this Temple University jazz show at night. Rich understood all the dimensions of the world, including the one I grew up in. He knew how I carried that in my attitude and my artistry, but he was confident and brave enough to wrestle and push me to keep growing.

Rich would be a massive influence on The Roots for the rest of our careers. Plugged in to the local circuit of poetic genius, Rich's connections allowed us to establish a presence on the Philly jazz and poetry scene alongside many of the greatest minds of our time. Amiri Baraka, Sonia Sanchez, Ntozake Shange, Ursula Rucker, Jill Scott: we were lucky enough to share the stage with these icons, crossing paths at Philly venues like the 40th Street Underground or the Painted Bride Theatre. Philly for us was becoming a self-fulfilling prophecy: there were so many brilliant artists in and around the city at that time whose careers were taking off, people who went on to become national and global icons, that it affirmed our vision of what was possible for us. The era was lightning in a bottle, but it felt absolutely organic. All these geniuses just felt like friends. Sonia Sanchez was just Sister Sonia from Philly. Ntozake was this Afrocentric writer jawn.

It sometimes blows my mind to look back. Like, *My god, that was Amiri Baraka. Amiri Baraka!*

Even though we were gaining popularity in Philly, we were reluctant to record a real demo. Malik had a friend named Jamaaladeen Tacuma, who was a world-class jazz bassist and one of the flyest dudes in the city and down with the Muslim community. Jamaaladeen was also the face of this annual jazz festival in Germany. They ran everything by him and would look to him for direction on who they should book. After he heard us play, he said, "What y'all are doing is fly. I'll put y'all on. Let me introduce you to the Germans and see if they want to book y'all for this gig. They need some new artists." And, ironically, the Germans came to Germantown to see us perform, sitting in our living room. We did a full-on performance of our entire set for just three people, who then offered us our first real gig. Before that, we had done local shows for $300 here or $400 there, maybe making $500 at most in one gig. And that was a lot of money, but almost all of it would go towards paying one or two classically trained musicians who would play with us. But the Germans came correct with what then felt like life-changing money. They said, "We want you to come and play at this festival and we'll pay you four thousand dollars, plus expenses." We were stunned. Their next question, though:

"What merch do you have?"

"What's merch?"

"What would you like to sell, you know, CDs, T-shirts, posters, stuff like that."

And we were like, "Oh. Yeah, we'll have that shit."

We instantly got to making iron-on T-shirts, the kind we could do at home, and then went to the studio and did our demo recording, *Organix*. Rich was also working, always knowing how to better leverage an opportunity. Patient in his dealings, strong in his character, and sound in his word, Rich did exactly what he said he would do from the moment he met us. We sat in his car one day, me in the front seat and Ahmir in the back, and he told us, "I'll get you a record deal in one year of us working together." And that's exactly what he did. He got that demo passed around, and soon we were working on our debut album and leaning on the creative community we'd found around us to add to our existing dynamic. Geffen Records signed us for our first major stateside release, *Do You Want More?!!!??!*, and licensed an EP called *From the Ground Up* through their U.K. subsidiary, a small label called Talkin' Loud run by legendary British DJ Gilles Peterson.

It was happening. We were conquering a city that was demonstrative in its disdain when pissed, but showed undying loyalty when in your corner. By the time any of us make it out of Philly to go on to other cities to try and blow up, we have established a base of support—in our peers and colleagues, our hood, our Philly families—that is unshakable. Nothing we face is a match for a praying grandmother who goes to church in South Philly every Sunday to call down protection on her grandchild. No critic can ever top the way your father or your mother critiques your art when you're back home in the living room. Winning over a crowd in Philly gives you the endurance to go make a thousand non-English-speaking Germans appreciate your flow. When you're triumphant in, for, and with Philly, the city won't let you forget that. At least not until you let them down.

That core support meant so much. Early on we were at a disadvantage because we played live instruments and nobody was really there for that. But then at some point in our career, having stuck to our vision of how we wanted our sound to feel and the musicality of our band, the tide changed. It became the standard to have live instrumentation, and you were wack if you just came out with a DJ. That was the era of other rappers reaching out to use the Roots band, but they would always be just super nervous about letting me rap: "Do you think we could give y'all the money and we just use the band because if you let Black Thought come out, I'm going to look like a fucking fool." It was a real concern that people had. When fans or reporters asked how come Eminem and Jay-Z have used the Roots musicians for performances that I wasn't a part of, that's why: Why would they want me to come and upstage them? For me, as long as the check cleared and I wasn't cut out financially, I was fine. I was still making money, and there was some internal validation that I got from knowing that a peer was making that decision in fear.

My mother would have loved all of this. She would have been on the road with us. She would have been in the studio with us. I've performed with so many of her favorite artists—folks like Gil Scott-Heron and The Last Poets—people that she used to rock *hard* to, who I've shared the road and the stage with as peers. My mother never heard what we created as The Roots. Not a song, not an interview, none of our gigs. But I have to believe she heard that demo tape in my boom box that got stolen.

I did it all for her. For her, I saw it through.

EPILOGUE: THE UPCYCLE

THE DALAI LAMA HAS SAID THAT DEATH EITHER STOPS you in your tracks or becomes the fuel that drives you forward. It can put a battery in your back or remove every charge left. Losing my mother was my greatest motivation, but it was only one of so many losses. The loss of childhood innocence in the face of lurid violence. The loss of a neighborhood and city that once held hope but came to harbor fear. The joy I felt in my youth so quickly snatched away and replaced with the responsibilities of an adult. I was grieving numerous losses, simultaneously. Everyone's life is defined by a constant state of change, but what does it mean when those changes all come with cortisol-spiking traumas, death, and loss? How can those losses become fuel and motivation? How do we embrace the sacred Life/Death/Life* cycles and see death not as a hard stop but as the needed compost for new growth? That is the essence of the upcycle.

My children haven't faced the same trials that I have,

* The Life/Death/Life cycle is a phrase coined by Clarissa Pinkola Estés to describe the rhythmic nature of love and life in her book *Women Who Run with the Wolves: Myths and Stories of the Wild Woman Archetype.*

which has helped me appreciate the roughness of my life in a different way. There's an edge, a certain level of hustle and self-sufficiency in me that I wish my kids shared. But on the flip side I wish I had the confidence and social skills they've gotten from having two parents both on call, or living in the home that they know they can count on. The freedom they have to grow naturally into themselves. It's a privileged existence, in my eyes, but a blessing to which they're oblivious. I wonder sometimes how to give them a broader experience. How to make them see life at the other end of the spectrum—the life that I had, where instability is the norm, hunger and hustle go hand in hand, and the stakes are high every day. Where scarcity and lack can be alchemized into expressive joy, where chaos is a classroom and love is found in the calm. And the calm is never taken for granted.

That experience produces someone like me, eternally restless, almost incapable of contentment. It just is what it is. The hunger is how I survived, but a hunger that strong is never satisfied. There is part of me that is always striving for *bigger better greatest,* the next achievement, the one that will finally fulfill me. I wonder if that feeling, that bottomless hunger, is still the hunger of a six-year-old kid desperate to remake the idyllic world he'd burned to the ground.

What if the hunger persists because I can't remake that world? What if my life will never be good enough because she's not here? She was my entire world.

I WATCH MY DAUGHTER carrying the same traits as my mother, her namesake: stubborn to a fault, beautifully herself, a wild and expansive personality, a light that I don't ever want to dim. I look at her, Saaliha, and see so much of my mother in her, a resemblance that neither my wife, my other kids, nor Saaliha herself will know. Shawn can see it. Ahmir, too. But my mother haunts me through my daughter, a welcome presence and final gift to make sure I would never forget her. That spirit is also a reminder that there's an urgency to this life. As a parent, I can sometimes feel the same energy within me that drove my mother, that moved her to take us to Baltimore, to carve out her own space and freedom, to love me enough to both show up and stay away through her addiction. And as an artist, I feel that same urgent force—a driving desire to document all that is still inside me, to make sure I don't take all of this music and these lyrics and these ideas with me to the grave.

THAT'S THE THING—we never stop changing, and so the upcycle never stops either. We might repeat the patterns established in the gory glory of childhood for the rest of our lives. So, as I deal with the inevitable angsts of the present, I find relief in identifying the cycles, so I can start to break them. I look into the shadows of myself, at all that is dark and broken, and acknowledge them. And when those parts of myself rooted in my past lives can't be remade and reintegrated, I let them go.

Don't be afraid to sit with all the parts of yourself. Don't be afraid to bare your childhood to yourself and say, *Yes, here it is: this is the root of my evils. And still, I love the child who suffered. I love who he became.*

But just as you boldly and bravely examine those parts of yourself, identifying what's broken and releasing what doesn't serve you, at the same time courageously chase the pure and honest dreams of your youth. Believe in the possibility that you can be all that you always wanted. Give yourself the unyielding permission to become.

Trust the upcycle.

ACKNOWLEDGMENTS

TARIQ TROTTER

Thank you to my wife, Michelle, for her patience and support through this life and every creative process. To my children, Ahmir, Benjamin, Saaliha, Trevor, Jordan, and Tarik, it is an honor to be your father. Thank you for all that you have brought to my life. To the city of Philadelphia and the world beyond it, thank you for all that you have shown and taught me.

JASMINE MARTIN

To the talented Mr. Trotter for your trust and loyalty over the past six years. To The All, and the legions of the Light who protect, provide, illuminate, and guide. To my tribe that loves me unconditionally, Mom, Daddy, Lisa, Sissy (Sissy Bissy, you're my greatest inspiration and deepest love). To Team Trotter—Munir Nuriddin and Shawn Gee—who have made work feel both expansive and like home, and who share credit in the creation of this book.

To Chris Jackson, for your vision and your talents and this incredible opportunity. To One World, Random House,

WME, Carleen Donovan, Joshua Kissi, Najeebah Al-Ghadban, Amanda Murray, and every soul that contributed a piece of their life force to this project, making it all that it is. To all of our partners that are supporting this book's entrance into the world.

Finally, to every person who has held space and grace for me in this process, for a process it has been.

I thank you.

ABOUT THE AUTHOR

TARIQ TROTTER—aka Black Thought—is co-founder of The Roots and a multihyphenate creative who has quietly affirmed himself as one of the most prolific, prescient, and powerful voices in hip-hop. Over the course of his career, he has won three Grammy Awards and three NAACP Image Awards. Not only did he deliver eleven applauded albums with The Roots, but the group also joined *The Tonight Show Starring Jimmy Fallon* as the house band and beloved mainstay of late-night television for over a decade. More recently, Trotter's solo music career has accelerated at full speed with his *Streams of Thought* series, featuring pairings with legendary producers. *Cheat Codes,* his acclaimed collaborative album with Danger Mouse, followed, and in 2023 the album *Glorious Game,* with Leon Michels of El Michels Affair, received similar praise.

Maintaining this momentum, Trotter continued his creative renaissance as the main composer and lyricist of the 2022 Off-Broadway production *Black No More*. He also made his Off-Broadway debut starring in the production, which earned a nomination for Best Musical at the Lucille Lortel Awards. His command presence has seamlessly translated into roles in film and television, such as HBO's *The Deuce* and Lin-Manuel Miranda's feature directorial debut, *Tick, Tick . . . Boom!* Beyond collaborations with everyone from Eminem, John Legend, and J Dilla to Linkin Park, Logic, and Fall Out Boy, Trotter co-produced the multiplatinum Grammy Award–winning Original Broadway Cast Recording of *Hamilton*. Alongside fellow Roots co-founder Questlove, he launched the production company Two One Five Entertainment, home of projects such as *Hip-Hop: The Songs That Shook America* and *Descendant*.

Twitter: @blackthought

Instagram: @blackthought

ABOUT THE TYPE

This book was set in Sabon, a typeface designed by the well-known German typographer Jan Tschichold (1902–74). Sabon's design is based upon the original letter forms of sixteenth-century French type designer Claude Garamond and was created specifically to be used for three sources: foundry type for hand composition, Linotype, and Monotype. Tschichold named his typeface for the famous Frankfurt typefounder Jacques Sabon (c. 1520–80).